The Ways of an Eagle

by the same author

Highland Year
Highland Deer Forest
Wild Highlands
The Year of the Red Deer

(All published by J. M. Dent & Sons Ltd)

The Ways of an Eagle

LEA MACNALLY

COLLINS and HARVILL PRESS

London, 1977

ISBN 0 00 262208 4
Set in Monotype Bembo
Made and printed in Great Britain
by William Collins Sons & Co Ltd, Glasgow
for Collins, St James's Place and
Harvill Press, 30A Pavilion Road, London, S.W.1

To George Waterston, for so long at the helm of
The Royal Society for the Protection of Birds in Scotland,
and to The Royal Society for the Protection of Birds,
a body which has done fine work for conservation over the years.

My thanks are due to my friend Tom Wallace for his company and encouragement on many of my eagle trips, and to Mildred, his wife, for typing my manuscripts and also to Jim Brown, another welcome ally at times, and to my sons, Lea and Michael. Last, but most certainly not least, to the unfailing understanding of my wife, Margaret, without which this book would not have been possible.

Contents

Illustrations

Foreword

I have written this because of a consuming interest in the golden eagle. For many years now I have watched and recorded the nesting success and behaviour of four pairs of eagles in the western fringes of the Monadhliaths in Inverness-shire. In the book I refer to them as pairs A, B, C, and D. They hold adjacent territories in glens radiating from a huge and remote upland plateau of heather and rock, cut up into a positive jigsaw pattern by peat runners and bogs, a plateau which sees few humans except for shepherds and deer stalkers. For obvious reasons I cannot be more specific in identifying the area.

The eagle has held the interest of man since Biblical times, as we can see from written reference to it all down the ages. It also vies, in a purely Highland setting, with the red deer stag in being used as a clan symbol or badge. Yet by virtue of the blind self-interest of man the golden eagle in Scotland very nearly followed the sea eagle into extinction as a breeding species. The golden eagle is a First Schedule Part I bird, that is, a specially protected species. Strictly speaking a licence is required even to visit an eyrie. It is an offence to take, kill, or injure, or to attempt to take, kill, or injure an eagle, to damage or destroy its eggs or young. To wilfully disturb an eagle while on a nest containing eggs or young is also an offence. For bona-fide purposes such as research an approved person may obtain authority, granted by the Nature Conservancy Council, to examine or photograph the nest of a First Schedule bird. The penalty for wilful interference with the golden eagle or any First Schedule bird is at present £100.

In the long run however the well-being of a wild species depends not so much on legislation as on the goodwill of man as a whole. In the very many remote areas of the Highlands where eagles exist, protection as laid down by law can seldom be satisfactorily enforced without this goodwill. Sadly, it has not yet reached every part of the golden eagle's domain, where passions can still be whipped up dangerously between those with conflicting viewpoints.

The role of predator in Nature is an important one even in our day when we have destroyed or disrupted so much of the balance of Nature. Seldom in

Nature will a predator wipe out a prey species for in so doing it would sow the seeds of its own destruction. Indeed, since weak, sickly, ageing or simply foolish individuals in a species are the easiest caught, so any predator will tend to concentrate on these, leaving room for the really healthy to thrive. This we must try to understand, even when we are strongly affected emotionally by seeing the torn and bloody remains of such prey. Sentiment is essentially human, but so too is conscious cruelty; there is no place for either in Nature.

This book is based on a 20-year field study of the golden eagle (1957–1976), under licence I must emphasise. There have been innumerable thrills, disappointments too, emotional involvement, fears and frights, and, I hope, achievement. I have at times been lost in mist; drenched to the skin and miserably chilled by unseasonal snows and torrential rains; in danger, quite literally, of being swept away by swollen, raging burn or river; tired out to the point of exhaustion, and, very occasionally, sweat-drenched and painfully scorched by merciless sun on heights which offer no shade. Yet always the lure of the eagles held irresistibly strong.

My hope is that the reading of this book may lead to a better understanding of the eagle – not as the regal, imperious, wholly admirable bird of the over-sentimental, nor as the merciless, rapacious, good-for-nothing killer of the die-hard grouse preserver or sheep farmer, but as a bird, an immensely interesting one, which has a place and function in our countryside and a right to live in it. Ask anyone in Britain which bird and which animal typify the wild places of Highland Scotland and they will say without pause for thought 'Eagle and Stag'. The presence of both arouses controversy, and perhaps always will, yet without them the Highland scene would lose immeasurably. Is it vain to hope that, at last, most people in Britain have learnt to stop weighing, on a purely profit and loss basis, the right of such wildlife as still survives to co-exist with us?

PART I

Struggle to Survive

High, very high, so high as to be only a black speck even from the ridge, itself over 3000 feet, the eagle swept around in wide effortless circles, using the air currents of her true element skilfully without expending as much as a single wing beat. Beneath her was laid out a seemingly endless vista of narrow glens and rocky hills, burns winding their tortuous ways down the steeps to the larger ribbons of rivers in the glen bottoms, they in turn leading to the long, narrow black tongues of lochs yet lower down. Stretches of high-ground plateaus, a jigsaw of peat runners and rocky outcrops, held expanses of heather interspersed with aprons of matt-black peat, while tiny, jet-black lochans dotted many a hollow. Difficult ground to walk over but not difficult of scrutiny to the eyes of the eagle. A spy-glass would have revealed the black speck to be huge, even in the immensity of the sky, for the eagle's long, narrow, wide-spread wings had a span of nearly 7 feet, and carried a weight of 10 to 11 lb. The eagle's mate would be less heavy and slightly smaller as is typical in birds of prey. The bird's colour was a rather drab, dark brown, relieved by lighter areas of abraded feathers and by the gold head and neck, that gold from which the eagle takes its name and which varies from copper-golden to white-gold in individuals. A massive, hooked, slaty-black beak with crayon-yellow cere at its base, and piercing light brown eyes, deepset under jutting 'eyebrows', giving the eagle a perpetual frowning, imperious look, completes the picture.

This eagle was probably shaking off the indolence of a well-filled crop which a breakfast of a cock grouse had induced. Now she was hunting again. A slight hint of movement far below was at once discerned by her keen eyes and she went into a superbly controlled fast glide toward a rocky ridge. There she settled, in patient immobility, like part of the rock itself, to await any further betraying movement. Only the clear, liquid eyes seemed alive, and indeed they were alive to the slightest repetition of the movement she had first spotted from so far above. Half an hour elapsed and still the graven image sat, in cold inexorable patience.

Nearby was a water-filled peat runner, its banks perforated here and there by mysterious round dark holes, from which at times a whiskered, black, blunt-muzzled head with dark boot-button eyes peered out cautiously. Reassured by the silence, a water-vole about the size of a mole moved out just a little from the drain's edge, and, with curved, orange-coloured chisel front teeth began to nibble the grass. A toothsome morsel, but only a morsel; the eagle ignored it for the time being. Further out and lower down, on an expanse of long heather, came another slight stirring as a mountain hare moved out from its form, questing nostrils and slightly protuberant eyes alert, its short, black-tipped ears upright. Then, reassured, it dropped its head to the heather and began to eat. Further and further it moved as it sought younger, greener and more palatable heather. An almost imperceptible stiffening of the eagle signified her awareness that here now was prey big enough to provide a worthwhile meal for her, but prey which a premature move would frighten back to the shelter of the rocky cranny. Minutes passed and the hare, emboldened by the continuing quietness and enjoying its meal, hesitantly loped forward yard by yard on to the bareness of the short young heather. The statuesque watcher judged that her moment had come; the hare was far enough from cover and still feeding away from it. A push-off with powerful legs, which were feathered in creamy streaked-brown, down to the scaly, crayon-yellow feet, and armed with huge, black, curved and needle-sharp talons, a strong flap or two of the wings to gain impetus, then a fast silent glide straight for the feeding hare. With a loud plop the startled water-vole disappeared making spreading circles of water on the black surface of the peat runner. The sound brought the hare's head up just before the shadow of death reached it. It ran, zigzagging this way and that in its attempts to get to cover. With a leisurely beat of one wing, then the other, the eagle forestalled each attempt. It acted like a winged collie dog, keeping the hare to the chosen path. The hare, ears laid back, panicked and began to run erratically, but the winged shadower would not be shaken off. Suddenly, like a rabbit pursued by a stoat, the hare gave up and squatted motionless but for a betraying trembling, and began to utter a heart-rending squeal, cut short, mercifully, as without halting her glide the eagle dropped her hooked talons into the hare's body and, with the constriction of each massive foot, literally squeezed the life from its victim. Still gliding the eagle swept across the plateau out over the deep glen which cleft the hills, as she made for a favourite feeding perch, the hare dangling limp in her dropped talons. At about 5 lb, it was almost half the eagle's weight, but she carried it seemingly without effort.

A tiny 'tragedy', a small cameo of wildlife drama, had been staged. It was one which could well be duplicated throughout those parts of the Highlands where the golden eagle still exists and adds to the attraction of those wild areas which we are lucky enough to have retained in so small and densely populated a country.

The golden eagle is the largest and most impressive bird of prey that still breeds in Britain. A dead female eagle which I found in 1960 measured 6 ft 11 in from wing-tip to wing-tip, was $35\frac{1}{2}$ in long and weighed 10 lb. The three front talons measured $2\frac{1}{2}$ in in length over their curve, and the larger back one 3 in over its curve. From its tip to the tip of the opposite front one the span was 6 in. Each talon was needle sharp and it is with these talons that the eagle grasps and kills its smaller prey, by penetration and constriction. The large formidable-looking beak is primarily used in eating. The eagle tears its prey into pieces small enough to swallow, while holding it down with powerful feet, against the tug of its beak. Most of our golden eagles live in the Highlands of Scotland though there are three or four pairs in the hilly Border area, and, of recent years, a single pair has made history by nesting in the Lake District of England.

In the Highlands the bird of prey nearest in size to the eagle is the common buzzard, an impressive-looking bird if seen on its own but one which would be dwarfed if seen side by side with an eagle. The largest live prey a buzzard will tackle is a rabbit and then probably a young or in some way disabled beast for a full-grown, healthy adult is usually too much for the buzzard to handle. Set this against the 36 lb weight of a red deer calf seen to be killed by an eagle and the gap is apparent. Nevertheless the buzzard is commonly mistaken for the eagle by visitors to the Highlands, deluded by its apparent size and their own over-weening desire to go back South and be able to say they have seen an eagle. A common report is of 'an eagle sitting on a telegraph pole down the glen'! I would go so far as to say that if you see an 'eagle' perched on a roadside telegraph pole it is a buzzard. Buzzards commonly use these as observation posts from which to swoop on mouse or vole below; I have yet to see an eagle on a telegraph pole and quite frankly I never expect to. To emphasise the very real disparity in size and weight of buzzard and eagle, a buzzard I measured was 3 ft 9 in from wing-tip to wing-tip and 18 in in length. A full-fledged young buzzard I weighed in 1963, as it was ready to leave the nest, weighed 1¾ lb. In the same year an eaglet at the same stage weighed 9¾ lb.

Seen in the air, however, with nothing but clouds to relate their size to, it *can* be difficult to distinguish an eagle from a buzzard. Where observers are desperately keen to see their first eagle mistakes are particularly frequent. The common identification formula that wide-spread, wing-tip primaries, separated out like the fingers of a hand, is the hallmark of the eagle is quite wrong. Both eagle and buzzard will show these wide-spread primaries, or, equally, primaries pressed tight against each other, depending on the particular aerial manoeuvre being executed at the time. A rule of thumb guide, particularly in summer when most visitors to the Highlands are out and about, is that the bird in the glen bottoms and seldom far from trees is the buzzard, whereas the raptor observed high above the mountain tops (and he can occasion-ally be seen from the road in some of the remote glens) is the eagle. A bird against the light of the sky is seldom more than a dark silhouette, colour indistinguishable, and the characteristic silhouette of the eagle is of a bird with a tremendous wing-span in relation to its body, lending the wings the appearance of a long, narrow, almost rectangular shape; the head is short and, the most revealing point of all, an eagle seldom flaps its wings when seen thus but most often sails along on wide-spread wings, using the air currents and thermals to glide with equal facility into the wind or down wind. The buzzard flaps its wings much more often though it too can glide and soar at times, even hover momentarily like a huge kestrel. In silhouette its wings look much stub-bier in relation to its body, wider and more rounded at the extremities. When seen perched, close up, the buzzard has an almost docile look about it, a round, brown, light-streaked head and a much smaller beak, in relation to the head, than that of the eagle. The breast and under-parts are commonly creamy-white, liberally streaked with brown and the feathering on the legs extends only to mid-leg, leaving exposed a short length of scaly-yellow bare shank. The eagle has a much flatter, almost reptilian-looking head, golden-yellow in colour, with a very marked jutting 'eyebrow' over each deep-set eye which tends to give it an imperious look, with most certainly no impression of docility about it, and a much larger, jutting-out beak. Back and breast feathers are of drab brown with no streaking or barring to relieve this, and its thigh feathers, creamy-white and plentifully flecked with very light brown, extend right down to the foot, leaving no part of the shank exposed.

The buzzard is much more vocal than the golden eagle, its self-descriptive mewing cry being well known to most naturalists. By comparison the golden eagle is silent indeed, its voice very seldom heard once it is adult. Over a lifetime spent mainly in the Highlands I have heard an adult eagle give tongue only some half a dozen times, and these, with one exception, were when I was at an eyrie. The first occasion I heard it was in 1959, in a lonely glen miles from any habitation and when I say that at first I thought it was an excited terrier yelping and actually scanned the glen from my aerial perch at an eyrie for keepers and their terriers, engaged on a round of fox-dens, you will realise that there can be no better description of this particular eagle cry than to liken it to the yelp of an excited terrier, oft-repeated, as it chases something. Moments later however I saw the eagle as she swept by, and again I heard her 'yelping'. On two other occasions in that year I heard her yelping her disapproval of my presence at the eyrie. This infrequent cry is, I believe, one of irritation and ill-temper at the sight of something or someone unwelcome. That this particular eagle in that particular year combined yelping with swooping repeatedly at my head while I was perched rather insecurely at the eyrie edge, conscious of the long fall to the glen below, lends considerable weight to my belief. There seems also to be an unmistakably querulous note to this yelping cry. The other cry or call of an adult eagle that I have heard is one very akin to the soliciting-food 'cheeping' note which young eagles use both before leaving the eyrie and also after they have left it, but are still, at least partly, dependent on their parents for food. When I first heard this cry, in June of 1967, again I was at a loss to account for it, for I noticed it as I was lying motionless on a high-ground ridge, spying at deer. Then I saw the vocalist – an eagle, hunting, gliding low over the ridge and emitting continually this ridiculous, for such a formidable bird, cheeping note, reminiscent of very young chickens of the domestic fowl. Considering how silent adult eagles are I count myself fortunate that I have heard both these calls and was able to identify an eagle as having made them.

Golden eagles are without doubt long-lived birds, where they are allowed to be. One indication of this is that they are believed to be 4–5 years of age before they reach breeding maturity. Seton Gordon, in his delightful book *The Golden Eagle*, mentions an eagle shot in France in 1845 which had a gold collar around its neck with the date 1750 on it. This, he states, was reported in the *Aberdeen Free Press* in 1845. If the date on the collar of what was presumably an escaped eagle, possibly at one time used in falconry, referred to the year of its capture then it would seem this eagle was 95 years old. Yarrel (*British Birds* Vol. 1) cites a golden eagle reputed to have lived in captivity for 104 years in Vienna. No authentic record seems to exist of the life-span of a wild golden eagle and this is not difficult to understand in view of the problems posed. Though eagles in our present times may have more chance of living out an allotted span, few pairs in the past were allowed this, and even today, in areas where there is little or no direct persecution, eagles probably fall victim annually to traps or poison, illegally used to get rid of fox or hooded crow. I believe that it is quite within the bounds of credibility to attribute a life-span of 40–50 years to an eagle but probably few attain this living wild, for, quite apart from the ever-present hazards of human interference, their day-to-day existence is rigorous enough, even though they are well equipped for it, to weed out all those who are losing their strength and vigour.

For such a large bird, in a habitat mainly of bare hills, wide views and clear skies, the golden eagle can be tantalisingly elusive, particularly in summer when most of our visitors to the North brave the hills – and so often leave disappointed in not having seen either eagle or deer. Even to those of us who spend a great deal of our time out on the hill the chances of seeing eagles are far better in the short daylight hours of winter than in the long daylight hours of summer, unless one knows of, and watches regularly, an eyrie in use. Neither eagles nor deer live by the clock; they begin their day at first light and in summer this is hours before most humans are stirring. By that late hour the deer will be lying restfully, chewing the cud of their early morning grazing, tucked into nooks and crannies in the high ground. Similarly the eagle, unless it has been unlucky, will be perched replete, digesting the result of its hunting or resting from its duties to the young on some favourite cliff-face ledge, motionless, and wellnigh impossible to spot. Summer is a rich time for predators with so many young and inexperienced birds and beasts starting out on life's adventure. The favoured daylight perching place used by a female eagle in summer once the early duties which tie her to the eyrie – incubating and brooding the eaglets – are over, will probably overlook her eaglet-occupied eyrie so that she can keep an eye on it. Her powers of flight are such that she can cross the whole width of a glen in seconds.

Quite a few of the eyries I know of in the Highlands could be walked into by a hill fox (or wild cat for that matter) and there is very definite animosity between eagle and fox. Each will prey on the other's young, if opportunity arises, and an eyrie with prey lying on it surplus to requirements could waft enchanting odours to a hungry fox. Enticed thus, the fate of the defenceless eaglets is not difficult to imagine.

A preferred perching place, used perhaps by generations of eagles, may be a cliff nook or a recess rather than an open ledge, in which an eagle is surrounded by rock on three sides and by an overhang above its head. This will be so sited that it will afford shelter from any wind, and certainly some measure of protection can be attained in all weathers. Evidence of such ledges can sometimes be seen by the presence of downy feathers, preened by the perching bird, clinging to any vegetation on the lip of such a place, or on the slope below. Occasionally the lucky find of a huge primary feather tapering at its point (I have one of $22\frac{1}{2}$ in), or of a round-ended tail feather a mere $13\frac{1}{2}$ in long, may betray a roosting place. Castings, or pellets, may also be found, ejected through the beak by eagles and other birds of prey. They are composed of indigestible matter which, if broken down, will give indication of the eagle's recent diet. Claws or beaks of grouse or ptarmigan, chisel teeth of black water-vole, fur of hare or rabbit, hair of deer or wool of sheep carrion, all can be traced in these castings. While the castings of small birds of prey such as kestrel or owl can well be descriptively called 'pellets' those of eagles hardly qualify thus, the largest I have seen being over six inches in length and the thickness of a man's thumb.

The present informed estimate of the number of breeding pairs of golden eagles in Scotland is no more precise than between 250–300 pairs, with a further number of single (that is unmated) and mainly immature birds forming a wandering population without regular breeding territories. From these wanderers, as they come of age, will be recruited replacements for the survivor of a mated pair, in the annual wastage. Seldom is a regular breeding glen left with only one eagle for long; in all cases I know of, a dead member of a pair was replaced by the following breeding season. Eagles mate for life and are territorial birds, but then, I believe, so are all birds – it is only that we tend to notice it more in the larger ones. Territory size, in my experience in Inverness-shire, covers about 10,000 acres per pair, but this necessarily has to be a fairly elastic estimate. Three of the pairs I have studied must at times overlap in their hunting area, on a huge, sprawling, peat hag plateau, from which their nesting glens, among others, radiate. But the actual nesting glen and hunting area immediately adjacent is held sacrosanct to the pair in occupation. It could also be logically surmised that where both prey and suitable eyrie sites are plentiful, territories might be smaller than where the reverse holds good. Be that as it may a resident pair of eagles will not tolerate the continual presence of a strange eagle on their immediate home ground; even their own young have to leave in the autumn following their rearing and fledging. Whether actually driven out, persuaded to leave, or just gradually imbued with the wanderlust of youth remains surmise at present.

Though tremendously powerful, impressive in size, and with an absolute mastery of the air currents and thermals, the eagle is not as adept and speedy in last-minute aerial manoeuvre as many of our smaller raptors, or even corvids or gulls. I have seen eagles mobbed by raven, hoodie, kestrel, and even common gull and, apart from poking its head upwards and gaping its beak in irritated threat display, it seemed to know it could do little against these smaller, agile birds which moreover can only annoy it. Once, a close friend of mine saw an eagle which was being mobbed by a raven, flip quickly and adroitly over on its back and it may be that in doing so it simultaneously thrust out and up with a taloned foot in an attempt to catch the raven that was flying so closely as to be almost on its back. I myself watched an eagle lose patience with a hooded crow which had been mobbing it persistently, and dramatically reverse the role, from attacked to attacker. Suddenly, it was the hoodie squawking aloud in terror. Nevertheless, a true corvid, it retained its wits. Time after time the eagle swooped; the fleeing hoodie could not match its speed of flight, yet each time at the last vital second it jinked with a side slip of wing, and the huge eagle thundered by, dropping far below the hoodie before it could pull up and regain height for another swoop. I have little doubt it could have eventually worn down the terrified crow but at last the eagle lost interest, and going into a long, fast glide, rapidly disappeared over the ridge across the glen, leaving, no doubt, a very thankful hoodie. This indeed is the way most of these encounters end, the eagle becoming bored with the smaller tormentor (which may be defending an aerial territory near its nest), and, setting its wings, goes into a glide which reveals just how fast this bird is by leaving its pursuer, wings flickering frantically, far behind in seconds.

In *Days on the Hill* by 'An Old Stalker' an account is given of an eyewitnessed tussle between a peregrine falcon and an eagle in which the falcon was the aggressor. 'The movements of the eagle were slow and cumbrous compared with the rapid motions and lithe activity of his adversary. Every time he dodged the eagle's stroke and wheeling rapidly got in his blow before the huge bird could recover.' Then, 'Finally he took to flight. With half-extended, half-curved wings he cleft the air straight as a bullet. The falcon pursued but being left hopelessly behind soon gave up the chase.' The peregrine falcon is generally reckoned to be one of the fastest fliers among our birds of prey, yet here was an eagle easily outstripping it.

There is little doubt that numbers of golden eagles are much lower than they were 100 years ago, yet at least they did survive a period of about 200 years of persecution whereas the sea eagle, closely akin in habit and size, did not survive. When one realises the extent and mixed motives of the persecution which took place from the late 1700s until the Second World War, and still continues sporadically in some areas despite protection, one marvels that the golden eagle did not follow the sea eagle into extinction as a native breeding species. Although the golden eagle is now on the 'strictly protected' list (a licence is needed even to visit an eyrie) clandestine persecution continues because of a small intransigent group of diehards. At times, mainly in the North-East Highlands where grouse are still significant as sporting birds, it is because of the alleged effect of eagles on grouse, although, in reality, eagle predation of grouse can be downright beneficial in its weeding out of the unhealthy element in the stock, for these are of course the easiest to catch and are inevitably the ones preyed upon. In the North-West Highlands persecution is usually carried out by those with hill sheep interests because of alleged harm to the stock by predation on lambs. The remarks concerning grouse apply equally, indeed more so, to the taking of lambs for there is no doubt whatever that a large proportion of the lamb remains that may be found at an eyrie are picked up as carrion, already dead from natural causes or accident. In 1973 the two eaglets in an eyrie which I was studying were killed, at around one month old, between two of my visits. I found them lying dead where they had been thrown from the eyrie after they had been killed. The rotten and highly odorous hind-leg of a lamb lay on the eyrie. Because of this, probably, the two young had been killed. In 1974 I found two domestic hen's eggs, which had been liberally poisoned with Phosdrine, placed as bait no more than 100 yards from an eyrie, actually at a little knoll which the eagle used as a perching place. Of the four pairs I began watching in 1957 intermittent persecution continued as a significant danger until the early 1960s. In 1957 the female of one pair was shot while incubating; the female of a second pair was shot at the nest in 1958, 1959 and 1962; in 1961 the female of a third pair was shot on the nest while it contained a newly-hatched eaglet and an egg near to hatching. The fourth pair's female did not go unscathed either in that period for she was, in one year, shot as she came off her eyrie and, in another, her successor was caught in a trap, probably set for fox. Since then, however, with the disappearance of the old school of keeper who saw no good in any bird with a hooked beak, direct persecution has been much less evident in that area. The climate of opinion, with the spread of at least relatively informed knowledge of the ways of birds of prey, is today very definitely more in favour of the continued presence of the eagle than it was even comparatively recently.

The 1800s, particularly the latter half, were critical for many birds of prey, as is quite evident if one reads books written around that period by authors who, paradoxically, were often field-naturalists of no mean knowledge. Charles St John, John Colquhon, Osgood MacKenzie, all had their share in and wrote about the killing of eagles and the collecting of clutches of eggs and mounted specimens of birds. The Highlands were becoming more easily accessible, indeed fashionable, and afforded a hitherto almost untapped source of sport, and also a happy hunting-ground for naturalists, many of whom had as a main objective the amassing of specimens. Collecting specimens at a time when the wild-life of the Highlands was extremely prolific was an unfortunate activity for which the individual was less to blame than the general attitude of the period. Both hill sheep farming and sport, mainly grouse shooting, also increasingly played their part, and here persecution was even less worthy in motive than that of the naturalist/collector. Fire-arms consistently improved and were more readily available; other methods of killing birds of prey, such as trapping and the use of poison, intensified and the hunters became more skilled with experience. A list of prices offered for the eggs of certain birds of prey in 1837 reads: golden eagle 23*s*., osprey 7*s*. 6*d*., sea eagle 4*s*. 6*d*., peregrine 6*s*. It seems that the eggs of the golden eagle held their value well (and 23*s*. was a considerable sum then) for Charles St John writes of them as being worth 'a guinea each in 1851'.

In Edward Ellice's *Placenames of Glengarry* a 'vermin' list is given for Glengarry, Inverness-shire, for the years 1837–1840, in which fifteen golden eagles are listed as killed, and twenty-seven sea eagles. The same book lists 'vermin' killed in the Glenquoich area of Inverness-shire (a much smaller area) between 1843 and 1862; thirty-nine eagles were killed (no distinction was made between golden and sea eagle), and in all likelihood they would have been mainly females at known eyrie sites. This type of persecution, recorded from only one relatively small area of the Highlands, was probably being carried out through most of the Highland area. It would be no exaggeration to say that where eagles were persecuted, either from the conviction that they were harmful to man's interests or for the motive of gain, in an epoch in which silver was scarce in the Highlands and selling eggs or birds for mounting was profitable, few known pairs were left in peace during their annual breeding period. At the least the female and her clutch would probably die; she was always the most vulnerable because of her stronger devotion to her nest. At the worst both adults and their young must have died. It would seem from contemporary writings, and also from the comparative prices of the eggs in 1837, that the sea eagle was then the more common of the two species, yet it eventually died out while the golden eagle survived. Colquhon in his *The Moor and Loch*, published in the 1870s, writes of 'the luxury' of seeing sea eagle and golden eagle nesting on adjacent sites on Rannoch Moor and writes that the sea eagle is far better known. Was it then more easily located on its nesting sites, more evident at all times of the year, and less wary than the golden eagle? Or is it that there was no longer room, in a more 'civilised' Highlands, for two species of large eagles, and did the less adaptable one succumb? One could almost draw a parallel between polecat and pine marten in this respect, for in that same period both these members of the weasel family similar in size existed side by side in the Highlands, yet the polecat disappeared as a breeding species, while the pine marten is still with us.

It is extremely ironic to reflect that the worst potential risk the species suffered, since intensive direct persecution declined, was in the early 1960s when it was realised that modern chemical seed-dressing and pesticides were very seriously affecting peregrine falcons and sparrow hawks, through chain reaction in their natural prey of smaller birds, and that something similar appeared to be affecting the breeding success of eagles, more especially in the North-West Highlands. The cause, puzzling at first, was finally attributed to the use of chemicals in modern, more sophisticated sheep dips. In eating carrion, which forms a very significant part of eagles' diet in the North-West Highlands owing to the comparative scarcity of grouse and mountain hare, eagles ingested harmful residual amounts. Of my four adjacent pairs two appeared markedly more affected than the other two and each, strangely, was on opposite perimeter areas, while the two whose breeding success continued more or less as usual (except in years of direct killing by man) were those in the central area of the four territories. Even more strangely, the latter two pairs were those which suffered most from the direct persecution still present until 1962. One of these pairs (pair B) had the female shot annually from 1957 to 1962 except when a third site, not discovered by the persecutors but known to me, was used. The same happened to pair C – luckily they too acquired a hidden site on their territory. The conclusion I tentatively arrived at was that, in the replacing of these older females around the early 1960s (who may have been ingesting harmful residues through eating dead sheep over a period of years) by younger females who had had less years of exposure to this new risk, the persecutors might actually have done more good than harm. From the recorded data I have the two pairs most intensively persecuted, pairs B and C, had far better breeding success than the other two pairs, pairs A and D. Pair A reared one eaglet in 1958, 1959 and in 1961, then one addled egg in 1962; she didn't lay again until 1968, again one addled egg; she reared one young in 1969, then no laying at all in the intervening years, until 1974, when one young was hatched but had disappeared a fortnight later. This means four young have been reared since 1957. In the same period the female of pair D reared one eaglet in 1959 and 1960, was shot in 1961 and her successor reared one young in 1962. Since then there has been a succession of dreary years of non-success, eggs always addled. In 1973 and 1974 she ceased laying at all. Thus only one has been reared since 1960. In comparison, pair B, whose female was shot in 1958, 1959, and 1962, has reared fourteen young since 1960, but in 1972, 1973 and 1974 she laid addled eggs. In 1975 she reared one eaglet and in 1976 she did not lay at all. Pair C's breeding success in 1961 is unknown but from 1962 until and including 1976 she has reared twelve young. Why this difference between pairs A and D on the one hand and pairs B and C on the other, seven in total for the first two pairs, twenty-six in total for the second two pairs over a comparable period and over comparable terrain? (See Appendix tables for full record.) All addled eggs collected and analysed subsequently were found to have traces of chemical residues.

Luckily the severity of the situation was realised and agreement was reached whereby the dips which contained the harmful residues were withdrawn. Was it in time for all eagles however, or are some older birds non-successful breeders for life, sharing a non-productive territory with their mate until they die and are replaced by a new female capable of successful breeding? Is there some unknown cycle at work whereby only 50% of the eagle pairs in this fairly well populated eagle area are successful, under a population control system of Nature, and are the three years of non-success in the hitherto successful pair B, and the laying of one egg and hatching of one young by the hitherto unsuccessful pair A in 1974, the beginning of another balancing-out cycle? Only time may tell and I hope to have some years of eagle-watching yet, without human interference to influence the natural course of eagle life.

PART II

The Nesting and Fledging Time

Golden eagles, as a general rule, have more than one eyrie on their nesting territories, though occasionally the particular terrain may limit a pair to only one site, in which case, necessarily, it will be used year after year. Of my four study pairs, one, pair A, had no less than ten sites on either side of their long, narrow nesting glen; pair B had three; pair C had six; and pair D three sites. Over the years I have found that with each pair one particular eyrie is favoured most. I also often found that an eyrie which had been unsuccessful, for reasons varying from addled eggs or the young being killed, to the female herself being shot on the nest, might well be the one chosen again in the following year. This means, in the latter instance, that the new female elects to use the fatal nest, off which her predecessor had been shot the previous year. Which of the pair dictates the site to be used in any particular year I can only surmise; logically one would imagine it to be the female as the one most intimately concerned. Seldom is a nest where young have been successfully reared used in the following year if other nests are available. The theory has been put forward that the nest which has been occupied by young eaglets over a fledging period lasting at least ten weeks becomes so fouled by prey remains, etc., that the adults prefer to leave it to the cleansing action of at least two winters before using it again. I cannot place a great deal of belief in this theory. For one thing I have never seen an eyrie, flattened and tawdry as it is at the end of a season's use, so foul as to be unduly offensive to my senses. Even if some eyries were excessively foul the rains, winds, snows and frosts of one Highland winter would be adequate to cleanse it. Also I cannot believe the eagle to be over-fastidious, as at times it eats carrion so ripe that it is overpowering to humans. It is not correct moreover to say that successful parents never use the same nest the next season. In two of my pairs nests were used in successive years of successful rearing even though there were alternative sites available. Pair B, which has three sites, used their favourite site to rear successfully on in the successive seasons of 1969 and 1970 and pair C, with six sites to choose from, used their favourite site successfully in 1970, 1971 and 1972.

The nest of the eagle is usually a rather untidy-looking large mass of dead sticks and broken-off branches up to an inch in diameter, interspersed with tufts of long wiry heather, some dead, some plucked out in tufts by the powerful beak of the eagle. It is sited on a cliff-ledge or recess, in places which may vary widely from the absolutely inaccessible to the all too easily accessible. Tree eyries are sometimes used; I have heard of these in the North-East Highlands, on the Isle of Mull, and in Galloway, but in the North-West Highlands tree sites are very rare. Occasionally exotic material is found among the nest structure. I have heard of the crook of a shepherd, which had been lost on the hill, found later in the structure of a nest, and twice of a stag's antler built into a nest. Once I found a length of orange-coloured nylon twine, such as is used in binding bales of hay, intertwined in a nest, giving it a garish look. The structure is almost invariably such a broad one that the sitting eagle, ensconced low in its centre, cannot see, over its outer rim, the terrain directly below her, nor can she be seen from directly below. The relatively shallow cup in the nest's centre is warmly lined with an abundance of great wood-rush, moss and dried grass, sometimes with the addition of dried rust-red bracken or fern, the whole making a very soft and cosy centre in the huge pile of outer materials. The actual size and height of the nest is determined by the headroom above, for nests are invariably built under the shelter of a rock overhang, a very necessary detail in the inclement Highland weather. One site which goes to an extreme in the way of an overhang belongs to a Ross-shire pair of eagles. Their nest is in a horizontal slit on a cliff-face with no more than eighteen inches between the ledge on which it is sketchily built and the rocky roof of the slit. One has to worm one's way along to this nest on one's belly, and, even more difficult, push oneself backwards in similar fashion to get out. Here the actual nest is a very shallow structure of heather sticks and is given only the barest refurbishing when in use, confined, of necessity, to the re-making and re-lining of the central cup. Young eagles reared here must have a bad crick in their spines by the time they fly out from it. Perhaps even more remarkable is the fact that this same pair chose, in 1971, a tiny recess-like niche high on a tremendously steep rock-face, and used no outer structure whatever, simply employing a lining of soft material on top of the wood-rush with which the tiny ledge was clad. I am at a loss to explain what dictated this choice unless it was a last-minute one forced on the female, near to laying stage, by something going drastically wrong at her original site, such as I have found to occur in both Ross-shire and in Inverness-shire when a pine marten took over the sheltered eyrie of a pair of eagles as a lying-up place. In any case, on this inauspicious site one eaglet was reared successfully but I have never seen it used since. To my frustration the sheer cliff was so inaccessible I could not get one photograph of this unique nest.

The opposite extreme to the two sketchy nests instanced above was the favourite eyrie of my pair A. This was built in a short rock 'chimney', on a jumble of rotten rock at its base. Well sheltered on three sides, this was the nest with the highest structure I have so far recorded. It reached six feet, measured from its base to its top rim, before it collapsed in the gales of one winter and has not been re-used since – not by the eagles that is, but in 1975 I found that its remaining structure was being inhabited by a pine marten. This site was one which had obviously been frequented by many, many generations of eagles for its lower layers (into which the pine marten had tunnelled) was a tightly compacted woody mass with only traces of long-decayed and compressed individual sticks. Hopefully, it will be used again in years to come. Directly to the south of this tall eyrie was its antithesis: a nest so situated, in superb cave-like shelter, that I was told it held, when in regular use, 'a cartload of sticks'. It was built, under its deep overhang, on a slab of rock shelving so steeply outwards and downwards that indeed an immense amount of material must have been needed to build up this outer edge while its inner edge needed very little attention.

Invariably, near to the nest, often growing from its very ledge, sometimes part hiding, sometimes part supporting it, there will be a rowan tree. Its alternative name of mountain ash is very descriptive as it is so often found clinging to a rock-ledge, or jutting from a cliff-face high up in the hills, finding sanctuary thus from grazing sheep and deer. At times the slender upper branches of such rowans will be seen to be rudely torn by the adult eagle's habit of breaking off sprigs to decorate the eyrie. More puzzling is the occurrence of a plant which, in Inverness-shire, I have come to associate with eagle eyries: the flamboyant rose-bay willow-herb. I have never seen this plant grow high out on the acid hill ground except in proximity to, indeed usually directly below, an eyrie. It occurs below at least one site of each of my four study pairs in Inverness-shire and I am at a loss to account for its presence in these places.

A further intriguing point about the eyries of my four study pairs is that on three occasions, over a period of twenty years, a completely new nest was built and, stranger still, the pairs involved were A and C, those which already had more than the usual number of sites. Normally the golden eagle has a few established sites and restricts itself to these, so why did these pairs build new nests? In the first two instances which occurred, pair C in 1968, and pair A in 1969, the new eyries were used in only that one year, C rearing two lusty eaglets, and A rearing a single eaglet. Both these new nests have since crumbled away almost completely. The location of pair C's new site was outwardly most ill-chosen, being far more accessible and less secure from human interference than their traditional sites. And this is in an area where eagles can be said to be regarded with very grudging toleration. She elected to build on a ledge of a small rock-face above a regularly used fox cairn. This fox cairn was frequently visited, as a routine measure in controlling foxes, by people who were most likely to be inimical to eagles. A fox was indeed shot at this cairn in the April of that year, while the eagle undoubtedly sat on her eggs above, amazingly undetected.

The third instance of the building of an entirely new nest is, to me, even more remarkable, as it was built by pair A in 1974, within six feet of an existing nest in good repair. This pair had had no success since 1969 when they had reared a single eaglet. It was when I went up to check on the existing eyrie that I found the new one and the tale is best told from my notes of that occasion. 'I began to have doubts as to whether it was occupied as, with eyes fixed on its outer edge, I climbed the face to the eyrie. The final approach is very steep and I was giving my full concentration to hand-holds and foot-holds, until at last I stood at the edge of the nest. Empty; but I had hardly time to feel despondent for, as I was looking at the nest, an eagle took wing from, seemingly, almost below my feet. Unbelieving, I watched as she swung out over the glen, gliding below me so that I was literally looking down on her. She was a superb sight, with the high snow-patterned hills on the opposite side of the glen as backdrop. She seemed to be a youngish eagle, most elegant and handsome, not a feather broken-tipped, abraded or out of place, with a glossy head of dark gold. Still depressed at finding the eyrie unoccupied I did not realise why an eagle should have let me approach so near before taking wing, until, looking casually below me towards where the eagle had appeared, I found myself gaping, incredulously, at the bulk of a completely new nest. Built on the grassy hill-face, it was squeezed between this and the base of a large rowan which grew, only feet away, to the south of the original eyrie. It rested virtually on the ground, admittedly very steeply-sloping hill ground, at around the 2000-feet level. Disappointment was banished by a rush of sheer joy as I saw, in the warm cup of this inexplicable new nest, a single egg. Two strides took me across to it and there I heard the incessant, vigorous cheeping of a nearly-hatched eaglet. I was so anxious to let the female return to her hatching egg that I rushed down the steep slope, dangerously.'

A little later, from the glen bottom I was able, with great satisfaction, to watch the female swing in over the glen towards her new eyrie, and, next day, as I'd hoped and expected, the new-hatched eaglet, pink skin visible below the still scanty thistledown covering, lay in the nest's cup. Much to my disappointment the eaglet, the first to hatch in this glen since 1969, vanished at about a fortnight old. I was at a loss, then, to understand why the new nest had been built so near the existing one, or why the eaglet later disappeared completely. However, in the following year when I again visited the 'double' eyrie site I found very definite evidence of a pine marten's regular use of the older eyrie in the shape of a tunnel leading in through its structure which enlarged into a living cavity at its centre, and continued to the inner edge of the eyrie where a much-used latrine indicated that the marten's diet had been mainly of vole, and of deer carrion. On the actual platform of the nest a thick, snug carpet of red deer hair formed a cosy couch for use when the weather allowed. I now wonder whether both the construction of the new nest, and the disappearance of the fortnight-old eaglet, were due to the pine marten. Possibly the signs of it first taking up residence had caused the young female to build a new eyrie – but not nearly far enough away, and in due course the marten had had a feed of the all too vulnerable young eagle, for the pine marten is a resourceful and hardy predator which is currently extending its range throughout the Highlands. It is only in recent years that I have had proof, first in Ross-shire, then in Inverness-shire, that its range can overlap with that of the eagle. So far I know of only one pair of eagles in Ross-shire which has had an eyrie taken over by pine marten, and they have not used this hitherto favourite eyrie for nesting since 1970. In Inverness-shire two eyries on the same hill-face belonging to pair A, the six-foot-high collapsed one and the double one of 1974, showed definite evidence of pine marten occupation, probably by the same individual or pair of martens since the eyries lie only about a mile apart.

It is in late February or early March, after mating, that the chosen eyrie site will be rehabilitated. There seems uncertainty early on as to which site will be used for I have seen more than one site superficially freshened up by a pair, but usually only in the one finally selected is there much work done, the central cup really formed and warmly lined. The existing structure will have been a flattened, compressed platform, perhaps tilted downwards at its outer edge, left thus by its previous occupants after the long fledging period, and may also

be partly damaged by the winter's storms. In the repair of this platform, and the construction needed to form a new snug nest cup, the
outer structure may be heightened by a foot or more. Where headroom
is scanty however only the very minimum needed to form and protect
the sheltered inner cup will be added. The normal clutch is two eggs
but this is not invariable. In three of my four study pairs, pairs B,
C and D, the clutch was two, but I have never known more than one
egg to be laid in the case of pair A over a period of twenty years in
which at least three different females were involved. A clutch of three
eggs has been documented more than once but I have never witnessed
one. The eggs, laid from around mid- to late March in my study area,
are very large and may measure some 7½ inches in circumference and
be about 4 inches in length. In some cases one end may be tapering;
more often, in my experience, both ends are equally blunt. They may
be very variable in texture, from appreciably rough to an almost
polished smoothness. Variable too is their colour: they can be a dirty
creamy-white with hardly any discernible markings, or the same
ground colour blotched with a pale lilac-mauve, or even richly
coloured, blotched with a strong red-brown. A further variation is a
thick freckling of red-brown, almost like a gigantic robin's egg. This
colouring does not seem to depend on the individual female concerned but seems rather to vary from year to year in eggs of the same
pair. Could the variable shell-colouring be affected or controlled by
the diet or condition of the particular female at the time of laying?

The incubation period is a lengthy one; indeed, if one only calculates
from egg laying in mid-March to eventual fledging in mid-July, the tie
to the eyrie is an exceptionally long one for the eagle parents. Incubation lasts about forty-two days and in the case of my pair C, the pair
whose nearly consistent success over the years has led to my being able to
ascertain their hatching time best, the eggs hatch around May 4th–5th,

which sets the time of laying at around March 22nd–23rd. The earliest hatching I have known of was on April 27th, which would put laying in this case at around mid-March. Incubation starts with eagles as soon as the first egg is laid and in the case of a clutch of two a couple of days may elapse before a second egg is laid. This gives the eaglet from the egg which was first laid and hatched a head-start, as it were, and almost invariably it maintains this throughout the fledging period, often to a very noticeable extent. Eaglets are not noted for an amicable relationship while sharing a nest and more often than not the stronger survives while the weaker dies, often in the critical first ten days of its existence. As the eggs are very thick-shelled, with a thin but tough greeny-white membrane on the inside of the shell, the hatching eaglet takes quite some time to emerge from the confinement of its shell. I have only twice in twenty years been at an eyrie as an eaglet was actually hatching and both times I left quickly to let the mother get back.

Speculation still remains as to how much of the long incubation duty the male eagle undertakes. He certainly takes some share for I have been lucky enough to see a change-over take place. In 1962 I was shown that the male does feel very definitely for his unhatched progeny, even if only instinctively. I had heard that the female of my pair B had been shot as she was startled off her nest towards the end of her long incubation, when she would be sitting tight, about April 20th. At dawn on April 21st I visited the eyrie and found the body of the female below and to one side of it. Her head and both feet had been hacked off as trophies by 'persons unknown'. Sick at heart I made my way quietly to above the eyrie. To my very great astonishment an eagle was incubating. It could only have been the male, and I remained motionless for some time, looking down on him, admiring the light and dark patterns on his back and wings where feathers were abrading and being replaced. His head turned from side to side at intervals as he kept watch over the slopes below but he never looked up. I hoped he'd be lucky, but I doubted if he could persevere in the absence of his dead mate. If by some miracle he did hatch the eggs he could never rear the tiny eaglets. The dual role of food provider and that of brooder in the early days, when warmth and protection is vital, could not possibly be achieved by a single bird however determined. As it turned out he did not persevere. On April 28th the eggs were cold and deserted, a stray blade of withered wood-rush lying forlornly across them. I think I was even more bitterly angry as I surveyed the abandoned eggs than when I'd found the decapitated, mutilated female. So much for man's wisdom and enlightenment in 1962.

In May 1965 I witnessed an instance of an eagle's anxiety for his incubating mate and of the desire to warn it of danger from man. I had detected, using my stalking telescope, an eagle sitting on an eyrie on the opposite face of a glen. As I turned round to put my telescope into its case on my back I caught a glimpse of an unmistakably aquiline black shape breaking the skyline on my side of the glen. Another eagle, on guard, overlooking the eyrie across the glen. I carried on, down into the glen, across its river at the bottom and began the very steep climb to the eyrie cliff. Halfway up I halted to examine the eyrie through my glasses but, as I was below it, I could not see any sign of its occupant, nor could it see me. As I resumed my slow progress up, the eagle which I had seen on guard glided into view and came low over the nest, head bent down as if striving to communicate with the eagle in occupation. It flew eastwards along the face and alighted, in a throwback of giant wings, and out-thrust taloned feet, on a prominent rock. While I was climbing the final few yards this second eagle, anxiety personified, and airborne once more, passed close above the eyrie again and again, head bent down, keen dark eyes, clearly visible now, scanning me. The eagle sitting on the nest was either too obtuse or too devoted to take heed and leave the nest, and only came off when I was almost at it. On the nest lay a young eaglet and an addled egg. I removed the egg for chemical analysis, and later found, as was common in the 1960s, that it contained faint traces of chemical residues.

I experienced a further highlight of the early nesting stages in April and May 1964 when I was extraordinarily lucky in being able to watch an eagle, unsuspected and without benefit of a hide of any sort, serenely incubating on her nest below me. This eyrie could be approached from directly below, unseen, by working one's way up through the crag to the top. Crawling cautiously into position, eighteen feet above the eyrie, one could only see the outer edge of the nest because of the crag's overhang. Only by dint of lying flat and precariously craning out to clear the overhang, toes dug hard into the peat and heather, could one see the whole nest, and below it the rocks at the base of the crag. On April 12th in that year as I peered straight down at the eyrie the eagle was sitting on it, incubating. It was a tremendous thrill. As I watched her, she picked half-heartedly at some remnant of prey lying by her on the nest and at one point she half-raised herself off the eggs and disclosed that there were two of them in the clutch. I watched her until the strain of maintaining my outstretched position became too much for me. During my vigil she changed position once, turning completely around on the wide nest so that her head pointed now directly into the rock wall behind the nest. As she did this she re-arranged the eggs with fussy attention before resuming their incubation.

On April 25th I had the same exciting experience and again left quite undetected by the object of my admiration. By this date she was obviously sitting much tighter, there was an air of concentrated purpose about her. On May 3rd I was again ensconced above her and

40

she was sitting noticeably higher on the nest and held her wings very slightly, but perceptibly, out from her body as she brooded, not clasped closely to it as on former occasions. Now and then she shifted slightly upwards, as if being pushed by the two tiny morsels of down-clad eaglets, about 2 oz in weight, which the eyrie now held. A plucked cock grouse lay on the outer edge of the eyrie, the red 'eye-brow' still visible on his head, the only bit not plucked bare of feathers. At my visit on May 8th she was not on the nest and one of the two eaglets was markedly larger than its nestmate. By May 17th the smaller eaglet had vanished as if it had never existed and again I saw no sign of the female. My biggest thrill was yet to come, however. On May 24th the mist was so thick and woolly that I had great difficulty in finding the eyrie crag, huge and relatively isolated as it was. That day, lying mist-enshrouded above the nest, I had the unforgettable experience of seeing the female materialise out of the grey, clinging dampness, heralded first by an ecstatic cheeping from the single eaglet, then by a swoosh of her giant wings, to land on the eyrie below my staring eyes. The eaglet, now just beginning to sprout little black-looking dots of feathers-to-come on otherwise completely down-clad wing edges and rump, welcomed her avidly, but to its evident disappointment she had no prey. The mist which had concealed my outstretched figure from her normally all-seeing eyes was also concealing prey from her gaze, and the larder was empty till better viewing conditions would return. For some few moments it appeared as if the female was trying to soothe her hungrily-cheeping young one, standing over it, dwarfing it, almost hiding it from my view, caressing and preening it, delicately and tenderly, with the huge hooked beak so obviously designed for sterner employment. This tenderness being ill-received she turned to the rear of the nest and picking up a tuft of loose heather she stalked solemnly across the wide platform, all vestige of

41

central cup now gone, and re-arranged it to her apparent satisfaction on an outer edge. She resumed her caressing of the eaglet but like a spoilt child wanting a sweet and willing to settle for nothing less, it would have none of it. Twice more, like a house-proud matron, she fussily cast around her nest and re-arranged bits of heather before she took wing again, flinging off into the grey blankness of the mist. This eaglet eventually left the eyrie, fully-fledged, around July 16th.

In only one year of my observations was I able to use a hide and this was sited on a ledge, a mere six feet from the bulky nest. It was *in situ* for four years before the nest (unfortunately not a favourite one) was used. It was on 11 May 1968 that I was first shut into this hide and left to sit it out. The two white down-clad eaglets were just over a week old and I watched the larger of the two bully the smaller relentlessly, pecking viciously at whatever part of its body was in reach but most often at its head, which was already streaked red from this savage treatment. When the female flew in, in a flourish of back-thrown wings, she held a fresh green spray of rowan leaves in her beak. This she arranged on the nest before she settled down to a 45-minute spell of brooding. Now and again she drowsed, snapping into wakeful-ness as the distant barking of a shepherd's collie, gathering sheep far below, reached us. Cocking her golden head to one side, she listened, her piercing light brown eyes hard and clear as glass, until quiet returned, when she relaxed again. It was no surprise when on a visit a week later there was only the bully left on the nest. On 2 June 1968 when I judged the surviving eaglet to be around $4\frac{1}{2}$ weeks old, little dots of dark feathering were appearing on the wing edges. The male arrived while I was in the hide, a smaller, neater-looking bird than his mate. He carried a plucked grouse dangling from one foot and this he dropped on the eyrie ledge and turning, took off again all in one smooth action, not even glancing at the eagerly cheeping eaglet. In the absence of the female, who still tore up the prey at this stage of the eaglet's life, the desperately hungry eaglet tried, repeatedly but most ineffectually, to feed off the plucked grouse, most often pecking at the part which was nearest, but which was also the least rewarding – the upturned clawed feet. It had no idea of how to hold the prey down firmly in two braced feet in order to afford resistance to the tearing beak and so it remained hungry till the female arrived at last. Again she carried a small sprig of green-leafed rowan in her beak, giving her an incongruously festive look, and she arranged this before turning to the soliciting young one. Holding the grouse down securely with her huge talons she tore smallish morsels from it and offered them in outstretched beak to the eaglet who greedily pecked them as they were offered. The female's attitude was very tender as she went about her bloody task of rending the meat from the carcase. The grouse dwindled in ratio to the bulging of the eaglet's rapidly distending crop below its throat until this had become the size and shape of an orange. It seemed then that the crop could not hold any more. By this time the soft innards were exposed within the body framework. The eaglet leant forward and, while the female still held the carcase down, it pecked a little of the liver for itself, a gradual initiation of things to come. With half the grouse gone and the eaglet temporarily satiated, the female helped herself to a loop or two of the entrails before moving over to the inner edge of the nest. The now replete eaglet waddled grossly over to her and crept under her breast feathers to doze and digest in comfort.

For the first ten days of the eaglet's life the female will be in almost constant attendance at the nest. In this early period the full load of the hunting is on the male. He does this and nothing else: the tearing up of the prey and the feeding of the young is done by the female, as is common to most birds of prey. An old keeper once told me of shooting a female buzzard at a comparable stage in the development of her young. He left the young alone on the nest so that he might get a shot at the male buzzard as he came in with prey. He never managed to shoot the male and days later, utterly sickened, he killed the last young buzzard. The nest, after some days of hot weather, was 'a reeking mass of fly-blown prey and fly-blown young buzzards, who had died of hunger in the midst of plenty simply because the male had no instinctive knowledge of how to feed them, but kept bringing prey in, to feed young still incapable of feeding unaided on the banquet of rotting food which piled up around them.' I have never forgotten his description of the incident, nor the deep impression it made on him even though he was inured to regarding all birds of prey as vermin, only fit to be destroyed.

After this initial stage passes, when the tiny down-clad young are vulnerable to the extremes of weather, even in the relative shelter of most eyrie sites, the female will become progressively less tied to the nest. However, she will still spend much of her time on a suitably commanding perch from which she can keep an eye on the nest and (until the next milestone in the eaglets' existence, at about 7 weeks old, when they can safely be left to tear up prey brought in and so feed themselves) return to it to feed the young when she sees the male leaving prey. Until the young are able to tear up the prey for themselves the bulk of the hunting must be borne by the male, with occasional help from the female as opportunity arises. Even when the female is entirely free from the chore of tearing up prey and feeding the young it is my belief that she will continue to keep a watchful eye on the eyrie until the young are finally able to fly, and thus no longer vulnerable to resourceful predators like hill fox or, in the light of recent years, perhaps pine marten too. I know from experience that she will also attempt, in some instances, to guard her occupied eyrie against man, though this is indeed exceptional. Some eyries are quite invulnerable to predation, such as those on inaccessible precipices, but in my area these are rare and most of the eyries of my four study pairs could be walked into by a hungry hill fox. So the need for a 'guard post' exists and this duty is carried out by the female.

In the relatively short space of ten weeks the comical-looking newly-hatched eaglet with pink skin showing through scant white down, an over-large head lolling weakly on an all-too-thin neck, flaccid pale-yellow legs and feet curled under it, will grow into a fully-feathered, magnificent young eagle nearly 10 lb in weight – an almost incredible transformation.

For the first four weeks of their life the young eaglets will be clad entirely in white down, a much purer white than the dingy grey-white of young buzzards for instance. At about 4–5 weeks old the first sprouting of dark feathers becomes noticeable, initially on wing edges and on the rump from where the tail feathers will grow. At $5\frac{1}{2}$ weeks old the piebald stage is reached when the eaglet will look half-black, half-white, the black being in reality a very dark brown. At 7 weeks the now rapidly feathering eaglet is showing more dark brown feathers than white down, except for the still largely white head. By 8 weeks even the head is nearly fully feathered, and by 9 weeks old the eaglet, to the casual human eye, is fully fledged, except for sundry fugitive wisps of down in the sombre dark brown plumage. At 9 weeks old the crop is still conspicuously white when it bulges, fully distended, through the cloaking brown feathers, at the juncture of the base of the neck and the upper breast. By 10 weeks the young eaglet is fully fledged, a handsome glossy dark brown body, with a head and neck of coppery-gold. These coppery-gold feathers, lanceolate in shape and sometimes pale-cream tipped, are capable of being erected, as in a feathered ruff, when the eagle is alarmed or angered. At that age, the

young of pair C invariably make their first flight, usually around mid-
July. They then have a body weight of around 10 lb. Most eagles do
leave the eyrie at about the 10-11-week-old stage, though occasionally
a lazy eaglet may stay 12 weeks on the eyrie. The earliest leaving date I
have recorded over the years has been July 8th, the latest, July 26th, in
1962 and 1958 respectively.

The eagles' habit of bringing in greenery throughout the fledging
period to decorate the nest is well known. In some pairs this habit is
more marked than in others. More often that not a single spray of
whatever greenstuff is most readily available near the eyrie is brought
in. In most cases in the North-West Highlands this means a sprig of
rowan. However their choice of greenery covers a wide range: green
tufts of heather, blaeberry, crowberry and cowberry may be brought
in, Scots pine or juniper if in the area, dry green moss, or a trailing
festoon of sphagnum moss. I have seen all these, and, once a large clod
of grass, with earth still attached to it was brought into an eyrie I was
observing. On 10 July 1959 the nest of my pair A was re-decorated
completely as if a conscious attempt had been made to freshen its
browned and withered platform. Not a vestige of brown was to be
seen, so profuse was the covering of bright green moss, green heather
and crowberry, evenly distributed all over it. This was exceptional,
however, even in a pair of eagles which used markedly more greenery
than the other three pairs in my study area.

By the time an eaglet is between 7 and 8 weeks old its hitherto
cringing, shrinking-away attitude to human presence may change
radically to an intimidating display of gaping beak and outspread
wings, head thrust out at the intruder in vulturine fashion. A huge,
scaly, crayon-yellow foot, armed already with needle-sharp curved
black talons, may shoot out at an incautious or over-bold hand which
has reached out to investigate the prey lying on the nest. The eaglet is

now strong on its legs, and active, whereas in the early weeks of fledging the weak legs were unable to support its fast-growing weight so that it moved about the nest on the mid-joint of the folded leg, not on its feet. On 26 June 1959 I noted at an eyrie of pair A: 'The eaglet's head is now predominantly copper-gold, the feathers at the back of its head and neck lanceolate in shape and still appearing separate from each other. Half extending its huge wings it brought them in sharply to its body with an audible clap while simultaneously a cloud of fine dust mixed with loose feathers rose from the dry and tattered surface of the nest platform in the sudden draught caused by this movement. As I shifted a piece of heather near its feet, cannily using my walking stick, it struck out with a taloned foot, lightning swift and with tremendous force. There was an audible 'click' as sharp talons hit hard wood and the force used was transmitted in a tremor via the stick to my hand. I was thankful that I had not been incautious enough to use my hand to shift the heather.'

On 3 July 1959 at this same eyrie I shifted a grouse carcase with my stick. This time the pugnacious eaglet gripped it in one enveloping foot and, as I pulled it free, lunged out with open beak and managed to grasp it so firmly that I had to pull the eaglet off balance, before it would relinquish it. Two days later, this eaglet advanced to the edge of the nest at me, clapping its wings, raising the usual dust-storm, head and neck thrust out, beak gaping wide, the feathers of its mantle standing out separately and stiffly erect behind its threatening head. So near did it advance that it actually struck my shoulder with the hard edge of one wing as it again clapped wings in threat display at me. On July 13th of that year this bold eaglet succeeded in grabbing my cherished Weston exposure meter which I had, stupidly, rested on the edge of the nest. Successful in this coup it then retreated from me to the furthermost corner of the wide platform, hirpling comically with the meter grasped in one huge foot. Luckily I had the attached cord of the meter around my wrist and by pulling firmly and consistently on this, praying fervently that it would not break, I was eventually able to retrieve my purloined meter before the eaglet had tested its edibility. Thereafter I possessed probably the only Weston meter to have been 'in the hands' of a golden eagle.

By 27 June 1970, with many years of eagle-watching behind me, I should have known better, but on that date I noted: 'The fur-denuded haunches of a fox cub lay on the nest, together with a half-plucked young grouse. The two well-grown young simultaneously rose up in righteous protest, wings half-extended, beaks gaping, a silvery drip of moisture showing on the hooked tip of one, and, as I reached out an incautious hand to examine the prey, one of them struck swiftly with a taloned foot and left me with a rapidly reddening hand, small punctures oozing blood.'

At around this same age, too, wing exercises are increasingly and vigorously practised. Indeed the last fortnight on the eyrie before that first flight is one of increasing and perhaps impatient activity, as strength is developed in wings and legs. On 25 June 1961 I watched an eaglet doing wing exercises, extending its wings and constantly flapping them in 'dry-flying' practice. In 1965, on July 10th, I noted: 'The eaglet was doing wing exercises today, as, unsuspected, I watched at long range, using my stalking telescope. It was repeatedly half-hopping, half-flying, comical in its dedication of purpose, from one edge of the eyrie to the other, wings extended, flapping energetically, at times even raising itself slightly off the wide flat platform.'

From around the 7-week-old stage the young eagle is able to tear up and eat prey provided by the adults, having at last learned to hold it down with strongly-braced talons and rend upwards with its beak, in the continual bowing action typical of the feeding bird of prey.

Typical eyrie site in the study area

Golden eagle incubating

One egg was hatching and through the ragged hole in the shell
I could see the beak of the eaglet

Hatching time is in late April or early May. There may be an interval of 2–3 days before the second egg hatches

Female eagle with recently hatched young. She is almost constantly at the eyrie during the first 10 days of the eaglet's life

At a fortnight old it is still clad entirely in white down

Offering a scrap of grouse to the 4-week-old eaglet

At 5 weeks old dark feathers progressively
replace the white down. Fox cub as prey

7 weeks old – tearing up and eating, unaided,
the prey brought in by the adults

8 weeks old – very active and strong on its legs.
The head is now assuming golden-brown feathers

Close up of the 10-week-old eaglet's head,
keen eye and impressive beak

Prey is now simply brought in by either parent and dumped on the nest, the donor departing, leaving the young to get on with it. I watched an eaglet eat an entire three-quarters-grown young grouse on 13 July 1959 and noted: 'The eaglet grabbed the feathered carcase with an audible scrunch as the talons closed round it, and retreating a little from my odious presence at the eyrie edge it began to eat it. The grouse was securely held in the taloned feet with around 9 lb of eaglet weight firmly above them. The head was grabbed first by the huge beak and the eaglet gave it a preliminary gentle twist as if to gauge the effort needed. Then it pulled the head smoothly off and swallowed it whole. Next it picked in fastidious fashion at the protruding bloody neck-end thus exposed. Working downwards from this, the grouse held lying on its back, piece by piece was pulled off, sometimes a sizeable chunk, sometimes a mere shred of skin with feathers attached. All was engulfed alike in the enormous and efficient beak. An entire wing came off in one powerful wrench and the eaglet straightened up to swallow this awkward bit, but no matter how ludicrously it contorted itself, the wing just would not go down. At last, admitting defeat, the eaglet disgorged it entirely and holding it down with just one foot, he systematically picked it to bits and swallowed it in this way. The breast was now tackled and all of it went down, including the sharp-edged breast bone. The remaining wing somehow seemed more manageable than the first for it was devoured whole. A feathered leg followed, slipping down easily, the curved claws being the last to disappear. The insides, except for the entrails, quickly vanished and the leathery gizzard was picked to bits. There remained only one leg and the rejected entrails, draped across a piece of heather. The eaglet, obviously replete now, picked up the clawed foot almost absent-mindedly and with an air of 'Don't really want this' swallowed it. It then made a determined lunge across the eyrie at me, clapped its wings as in derision and then, as if with deliberate intent, turned its rear towards me and began slowly to elevate its tail. Realising what was to follow (the inevitable outcome of the meal), I jumped quickly aside and focusing my camera I was just in time to photograph the tremendous jet of white liquid which curved out over the nest edge into space – and which had apparently been intended to whitewash me.'

By the time an eaglet leaves the nest it is strong in wings, body and legs, profiting by the increasing activity of its last weeks on the eyrie. In a minority of cases an eyrie may be so sited as to allow an eaglet actually to walk out of it. Normally, however, the occupant must leave the eyrie by air, without any previous experience of that element. This being so it never fails to amaze me how skilfully eaglets manage their very first flight. Admittedly that first flight may not be of long duration, and of course there is still much to learn, but this launching out fearlessly into space is surely a major obstacle overcome. The first time I saw an eaglet take its maiden flight was on 19 July 1959 when I noted: 'The eaglet, standing on the outer edge of the dilapidated nest, with a half carcase of rabbit lying neglected on it, made a nervous, curtseying motion outwards, thrusting out its head and neck and dipping its entire body simultaneously, as if in pagan propitiation to some spirit of the air. Suddenly, it launched itself in one swift flinging-off motion from the edge of the eyrie, propelled outwards by the strong legs. The wings opened fully and immediately checked the dropping motion of the eaglet as they gripped, for the very first time, the air above the deep, shadowed glen. It glided out straight and fast without a flicker of the extended wings right across the gulf of the glen and then, turning parallel to the high rocky face on the opposite side, glided equally skilfully along it for some hundreds of yards, without a single wing flap, landing neatly with a throw-out of extended talons, on a huge upthrust rock.'

The stunning effect that the first flight has on someone who has not witnessed it before, was reaffirmed when I had a friend with me at an eyrie, on 16 July 1972. The eaglet launched itself as if it were absolutely familiar with this new element, wings out, primaries slightly curving upwards. Losing height a little, it banked around expertly and then, gliding parallel to the eyrie-face, without flapping a wing, vanished around a ridge to our west. My friend turned to me and in what I can only describe as a dazed, unbelieving voice asked, 'Was that the young eagle?' and I had to reply, 'Yes, it most certainly was.'

A nest, in its early days a reasonably neat and colourfully-lined structure with the warm cup holding the eggs safely in its centre, becomes a completely transformed, flattened, withered-brown platform, at times dangerously sloping downwards on the outer edge by the time its occupant flies. Innumerable small feathers, wisps of down, tiny fragments of bone, scraps of fur or of deer-calf hair are trodden into the withered surface. Ten weeks of occupation by increasingly weighty young, and the regular visits of the adults, has caused this compression of the nest. Large bones, such as the strong leg-bones and domed skull-tops of deer calves, lamb or fox are usually notably absent though all may have featured as prey. These larger bones are actually lifted and carried away by the female to be dumped, admittedly at times not very far from the eyrie site. I have commonly found such large bones on the slope below an occupied eyrie, but not so near as to have been pushed over a nest edge by an unduly fastidious eaglet. Surveying the empty eyrie one can readily understand why perhaps a foot of new structure is needed to restore a nest. It has to be strong and cunningly woven and wedged into its cliff-ledge to support the weight of the eagles and to withstand, winter after winter, the inclement weather of the Highlands.

Seldom do the adults show themselves when a human visits an eyrie.

A dark speck may be seen very high above, but more often the adults, the female in particular, will be watching from a distant perching point, themselves unseen. With one very marked exception this holds good for my four study pairs over the years. The exception was pair C where the female, in decisive fashion, showed that she was always on guard, appearing each time I visited an eyrie containing young of hers. Even more rarely does an eagle display any sort of aggressiveness and use tactics calculated to intimidate a visitor to an eyrie, or press home an attack likely to cause him injury. When one is experiencing such tactics it is difficult to judge impartially – this I can vouch for. Once again the female of pair C was the outstanding exception. However, the first time that I was the astonished and, frankly, highly apprehensive victim of such debatable tactics was on 5 July 1959, by the female of pair A. This is also the female I first heard uttering that yelping, terrier-like annoyance cry described in Part I.

On that day, while I was perched at the outer edge of an eyrie, with a long steep drop below it, I suddenly saw the female fly out above me, only to return quickly, flying with rapid wing beats close to the rockface. This time she was below my feet, so that, craning around, I was actually able to look down on her. She repeated this short patrol three times, each time alternately above and below the eyrie. Once I heard her give vent to her terrier-like yelping on an unmistakably querulous note as she flew by and then she stopped. Thrilled and delighted by her display, I promptly forgot her. I was soon to be forcefully reminded of her! I had resumed my attempts at photographing the large, 8-week-old eaglet and, balanced against the nest, was without hand-hold (both my hands being occupied with my camera) when she arrived again. My first warning was a terrific tearing swoosh of displaced air as she pulled out of her swoop directly above my head. It was so sudden and utterly unexpected that I almost overbalanced in

52

an uncontrollable jump of fright. She kept up her perpetual patrolling during the rest of my stay at the eyrie that day, twice more causing me to jump as she repeated her swoop above my head. She came so close that, looking up, I had a magnificent view of her massive crayon-yellow, scaly legs and feet folded up under her body. On July 10th she renewed these most intimidating tactics, but in an even more determined fashion so that I noted: 'Three times in a space of five minutes she repeated that swoop at me, the nerve-wracking "swoosh" every time making me instinctively flinch and duck, and pull my head in like a tortoise withdrawing into its shell. The last time she did it I looked up in time to catch her sky-blotting shape mere feet above. I thought of tales I had heard of eagles hazing panic-stricken red deer over a cliff edge to death below by similar tactics, and realised just how feasible this could be.'

However, I did not have to endure further ordeals that day for I next saw my attacker disappearing into the distance up the long glen, her yelping cry floating back to me. But why did she leave it till July to express her annoyance? She had seen me visit the eyrie on many occasions before that, and I made three further visits after July 10th fully anticipating a repetition of her attacks. But she never appeared, and the eaglet flew safely on July 19th, as related.

It was to be 1963, in a different glen, the territory of pair C, before I was again subjected to attack by an eagle, but you can read an account of this in Part IV, Observation Diary.

PART III

The Prey of Eagles

For such large birds living in a habitat mainly of bare hills where stalkers and shepherds, keen-sighted men by nature of their very vocation, are out and about for much of the year, there have been few eyewitness accounts of eagles killing prey. This prey, as recorded over the years mainly at occupied eyries, is extremely varied – one could say that anything remotely edible and within the powers of the eagle to kill is taken if the opportunity arises. The list of prey species I myself have recorded at the eyries of my study pairs is given in the Appendix. Where the mountain hare is plentiful this is undoubtedly the favoured prey, with grouse probably a second choice. Unfortunately, nowadays neither mountain hare nor grouse are plentiful in the North-West Highlands, although they are both still plentiful in the North-East Highlands. In the North-West Highlands, carrion, mainly in the form of dead red deer and hill sheep, forms an important part of the diet of eagles, distasteful as the thought may be to those whose image of the eagle is that of a regal bird that eats only what it kills. Carrion is mainly available in winter and spring, but it is also available at the nesting season of the eagle in the form of hill sheep which may die at the lambing time, and, of course, the appreciable numbers of weak lambs. There are also a few red deer calves which may die prematurely.

At different eyries over the years I have listed prey as small as beetle (beetle wing cases found in a casting of an eaglet at an eyrie of pair C in 1974) and as large as red deer calf and adult fox. At the eyries of pair

54

B and pair C deer calf featured regularly as prey from around mid-June until mid-July, when most of the eaglets left the eyrie. June is the month when red deer calves are born, mid-June being the peak period, and in the natural scheme of things, red deer calves in the first ten days or so of their lives are often to be found lying alone on the hill while their mothers are absent. This is entirely natural; it does not mean an orphaned or deserted calf, it is simply that the mother is away grazing, at some distance perhaps, depending on her choice of area, while the calf, still too young to accompany her everywhere, is left lying alone until her return at evening. The calf's protection then is in absolute stillness, lying low in whatever cover is available, most often long heather, the lee of a huge rock or peat bank, the shelter of the bank of a burn or among the long rushes of a damp flat. It is at this stage that they are most vulnerable to predation by eagle and fox, and by the remorse-less but wise law of natural selection those calves which choose their cover badly or are careless in maintaining stillness when danger is near are those which will be most readily detected and preyed upon. By no means every remains of deer calf seen at an eyrie implies a kill however; many will have been picked up already dead as carrion, weak calves which have died shortly after birth, or which have been born dead. There is, however, no doubt that an eagle can, and will, kill deer calves if the opportunity arises. There are enough eyewitness records of this to render it quite indisputable. Having said this the largest total of red deer calf remains I have recorded at any one eyrie, in a season, has been five, a very small percentage of the numbers of calves born in the wide area around that eyrie. Once the vulnerable period for the deer calves is over, they will accompany the mother wherever she goes, and will be under her protection. This does not mean that eagles will not at times attempt to kill such calves, or even adult deer, for this too has been seen, but I firmly believe it is so rare as

55

to be insignificant.

At the eyries of pairs A and D I have never seen red deer calf and they inhabit territories adjacent to those of B and C, with equal opportunities to kill deer. Pair D have had such poor breeding success over the years that prey observation has been negligible. Therefore from three pairs of eagles I can say that with two pairs red deer calf featured regularly each year at their eyries, and with the other pair, pair A, it never featured in my period of watching. Red deer calves weigh an average of 14–15 lb when born and this is one and a half times the weight of the larger, female eagle. I believe that while an eagle can undoubtedly lift such a weight off the ground, with the powerful impetus gained at the culmination of a long fast swoop, it cannot carry it far in sustained flight. In most cases, I am sure, the eagle, having killed or found a dead deer calf, will cut it in half by severing the spinal vertebrae at one of the joints and then carry half into the eyrie. This severing of the soft juvenile bone would be easy to accomplish, and is a method the hill fox also uses. Another way, which was probably employed in the case of the 1963 calf skeleton found on the eyrie of pair C (see Part IV), is when one or both adults eat sufficient of the flesh to enable the remainder to be lifted in. This is rare; I have only recorded it on that one occasion. In the majority of cases where deer calf remains have been seen at an eyrie it has been in the shape of hind-quarters or forequarters, or a portion of either.

I myself have never seen an eagle kill a calf but I have had first-hand accounts from reliable friends. I should perhaps state now what I have so far merely implied, that it is only when the hind is too far away from her calf to be able to defend it that an eagle has much chance of success in killing one. If the hind is near enough she will defend her calf indomitably even if she herself is in obvious terror of the huge winged attacker dropping out of the sky. If she is grazing too far away, and is therefore too late to save the creature's life, she will, drawn by its agonising, ear-piercing squeal, come racing in and, raging with irresistible maternal grief, drive the eagle off her calf's body, lashing out, ears laid back, with savagely flailing fore-hoofs, perhaps rising high on her hind-legs to do so. She may thereafter linger by her dead calf for hours, wondering perhaps why it does not waken, calling to it at intervals. I have myself witnessed a case of such hopeless devotion, and was first attracted to the hind by her periodic long-drawn-out bellowing call. There was no outward sign of injury on her calf and it was not until I skinned it that I found the distinctive talon punctures of the eagle along the line of the spine and at the back of the neck. In a case like that the eagle has only to wait until the hind finally gives up her vigil and leaves the now cold and stiff body of her calf, not a difficult task for a bird used to perching motionless for hours at a time on some favourite crag. It may not necessarily linger in the immediate vicinity but it will certainly return when the time is ripe to profit from its kill.

A friend, a reliable and very experienced stalker, vividly described to me the manner in which an unfortunate calf met its death. He had been out on the hill in June and was lying spying, with his stalking glass, at a lone hind some distance away which he suspected of having a calf hidden nearby. As he lay there an eagle suddenly appeared in his field of vision, gliding terrifically fast and silently on a downward swoop. A young, brightly-dappled calf sprang up from hiding and raced towards the hind. The eagle had it almost instantly, fixing its talons into its back and carrying it aloft without perceptible halt in the accelerating glide. However it was quite unable to gain height or carry it far and, having got the desperately struggling calf off the ground, had to flap its huge wings frantically even to keep airborne. Inevitably it had to drop the calf, which collapsed on impact with the ground but almost immediately struggled to its feet and again attempted to reach its mother, by now running towards it. In vain. The eagle in that short interim had had time to turn, gain distance, and go into another fast gliding swoop. The running calf was again scooped up off the ground. Once more the eagle had to drop the calf and this time it lay still; the eagle at once banked in and fixed talons into it. Both mother and my informant were by this time racing towards the hapless calf in a mutual and equally fruitless attempt to save it.

The eagle rose off the calf but in the short time that had elapsed it had already pierced a hole between the calf's ribs, and had exposed and part eaten the liver. The dead calf was weighed and it proved to be 16 lb. Little wonder the eagle could not keep it airborne, but what a tribute to the power and impetus of its swoop which enabled it to lift such a weight off the ground.

A more remarkable eyewitness account was told to me by another friend, also with years of experience on the hill. Remarkable, that is, in the size of the calf tackled and killed. He had been out on the hill when, not very far away but just out of his view, he heard a deer calf squeal – a piercing and far-carrying cry of anguished terror. Running towards the sound he was in time to see an eagle with its talons hooked fast into a large, dappled calf, which was lying stretched on its side, still kicking spasmodically. Simultaneously the mother hind ran in from another direction, wild-looking, her ears back, eyes rolling, spurts of water being kicked up by each plunging hoof from the boggy ground. She was too late. The eagle rose and departed and the hind ran about 50 yards off, then stood, a nervous fore-leg raised to stamp, nostrils flaring, watching my friend. The calf was weighed, and it scaled 36 lb and was judged to be 3–4 weeks old.

These are success stories but, as with all predators, the eagle is often unsuccessful. Tom Speedy in his book *The Natural History of Scotland with Rod and Gun,* writes: 'Some years ago I witnessed an eagle attacking a calf but the mother, attracted by its cries, ran to the rescue and drove it off.' Not such a dramatic story as that of the killing of a calf by an eagle, but one which must often occur where eagles attempt to take deer calves. More dramatic, but again failure for the eagle, was an eyewitness account, on the hills of Arnisdale in the Glenelg area, as told to me by a friend who had been a shepherd there in his youth. Coming over a ridge on a day in June, he saw a hind racing crazily along, nose pointing skywards, now and again emitting an anguished call. Then he spotted an eagle, wings flapping madly to maintain its course, flying along hardly higher than the desperate hind's nose – and dangling, kicking frantically, from its dropped talons was the hind's calf. Unable to gain or even maintain height with the struggling calf, the eagle dropped it almost on top of the hind. The hind at once stood over the fallen calf which was stirring feebly and faced up to the low-circling eagle, which however suddenly saw the shepherd hurrying forward and flew off. Before the shepherd got to the hind and calf, the calf had struggled to its feet, and, they too, now conscious of his approach, had gone. A very lucky calf, to have actually been in the grip of an eagle and to have survived.

Though I have never seen an eagle attack a calf I have seen eagles, in the month of June, patrolling areas where calves were being born daily and where others were, as is normal, lying alone while their mothers were some distance away, grazing. Once I watched a hind suddenly stop grazing, lift her head and stare fixedly at an object on a green. Watching from long range I could not identify the object and suspected it to be a young deer calf. The lone hind, head and long neck outstretched, advanced towards it inquisitively. The object took wing, and showed itself to be an eagle. Though there can be no doubt that some, if not all, eagles will prey on deer calves, I have seen hinds and their calves lying, or grazing unconcernedly directly below an eyrie on which there may have been at that very moment the remains of a deer calf. Where mountain hares are plentiful I doubt if any deer calves would be preyed on apart from a rare 'lucky' capture. On the other hand in an area like the island of Rhum on the north-west coast of Scotland, where there is virtually no natural prey for the resident pairs of eagles except red deer calves, carrion and sea birds, one could logically expect calves to be preyed upon, as indeed they are.

There have been reliable eyewitness accounts too of deer calves being attacked as late as October, the tactics of an eagle or a pair of eagles at this stage being to try and separate a calf from a panic-stricken hind by continually swooping at and hazing the running deer until the calf begins to tire and drop behind. When deer are subjected to a series of quickfire, low-level attacks, with that frightening swoosh every time an eagle pulls out of its swoop, they have every reason to panic. A friend of mine, while out stalking in October on an estate near Fort Augustus, saw an eagle use these tactics and eventually succeed in fixing its talons into the back of the head and neck of a well-grown calf, 3–4 months old. It was flapping its wings furiously in an attempt to keep its balance and to complete the demoralisation of the terrified victim. In that way, eagle still riding on the calf, they went out of sight before he could see the eventual outcome.

What I regard as the classic description of such an attack on a deer calf of this size and age was given by Henry Hope Crealock in his mammoth work *Deerstalking* published in 1892. I can do no better than to quote verbatim from this:

One lovely morning in September 1888, I sailed up in the boat to the west end of Loch Fannich. I found Campbell the stalker waiting for me, accompanied by a gang of men who had been working on the road to Loch Rosque. These men were on their way to Ullapool but instead of going straight on by the public path through the middle of my forest, as they had the right to do, they had been civil enough to wait till I arrived, and then come with me so that they would not disturb deer if there were any en route. Having thanked them for their civility, we at once started towards the Braemore march, the direction in which they were going. When we had got as far as the Fox's Den Coire,* opposite the Flucht Coire, I suddenly became aware of a large herd of deer high up above me. I tumbled off my nag into the heather and we all went flat; having spied them, we found nothing very good among them, and were about to proceed forward, when a magnificent golden eagle from the peaks of Coire Mhor swooped down at the herd, trying to strike a calf. He was a splendid eagle, I have never seen so large a one, and I never saw a bird in such perfect and brilliant plumage. He missed the calf, but, wild with terror, away rushed the whole herd straight down the precipitous slopes of the Coire, and in our direction. I snatched the rifle out of the case to be ready, but soon put it back again for the eagle, having missed the calf, wheeled up in the air screaming and was after them in a minute and again he singled out the calf, now straining every nerve to keep up with its terrified dam in her flight. This turned the herd from us, which scampered back up the rugged rocks as fast as they had come down. I never saw terror better illustrated; up and down, backwards and forwards did the poor beasts go, the eagle after them, but he would not be denied – he had made up his mind to have that calf and as he was always able to cut the herd off in whichever direction they fled he at last separated the hind and her calf from the rest of the deer. Now the chase became hotter and more exciting than ever. The panting herd, having a moment's respite,

*coire: large, semi-circular hollow in the mountainside, blind-ended
and enclosed on three sides by steep slopes.

stood at gaze, watching the wild efforts of the hind to save her calf from the deadly clutch of the monarch of the air. Constantly turning her head, she kept a watchful eye on her tormentor. She managed to dodge him yet for some time, though he made several ineffectual dashes at the calf. But, done at last, and utterly exhausted by her vain efforts to elude the attacks of the eagle, she took refuge against a pile of wild rocks tumbled down from the peaks above. There maternal courage and despair determined her to make her last stand in defence of her offspring which, half dead from the hunt and its terror, cowered behind its mother, bleating piteously, while all the little ones of the herd joined in the sad chorus.

The eagle, in close pursuit, came sailing with outstretched motion-less pinions down the wind straight at her – awful moment of suspense and excitement to all of us who were looking on – we were sure he would get the calf now. But no! The gallant old hind, panting and exhausted though she was, made one last fight for it. Well done, old lady! Well and gallantly done indeed! For, as in full swoop the eagle made a dash at her, up she went on her hind-legs and struck at him in the most vicious way with her sharp fore-hoofs and it was with diffi-culty that he dodged the blow. Baffled again he soared up the Coire, screeching in his wrath. This was the finest episode of wild nature I ever witnessed on the hill. I had my glass on them and could see every detail. The expression of despair and wild terror on the face of the agonised mother, her ears laid flat to her neck when she made that savage slap at her enemy, cannot be described – it had to be seen. The gang of men were in the greatest excitement and I observed that had they not been so civil as to wait for me, they would have missed one of the finest sights they were ever likely to see in their lives on the hills of the Highlands. The eagle continued his wheeling and soaring for some time and followed the deer to the high peaks of the Flucht Coire, but they kept close together, and never gave him another chance, so after a time he took himself off, though it was hours before the herd quieted down or would feed, standing with heads erect and straining eyes to see if he would return.

A spirited artist, Crealock included a remarkably emotive illustration of the final tableau, as he saw it.

Tales of eagles, alone or working as a pair, driving panic-stricken deer over a cliff are so often repeated in deer country in the Highlands that it is difficult not to place some credence in them. J. G. Millais, in his book *British Deer and Their Horns*, published 1897, gives a sketch of a hind panicked over the edge of a narrow deer path which crossed a cliff-face, falling to her death far below for the delectation of the eagle later. He writes:

In the inexpressibly wild and grand forest of Black Mount where eagles are now common objects is a narrow pass on the precipitous slopes of Clashven, much used by deer in winter, and, a hundred feet or so below this pass, James McColl, the stalker on this beat, has found several carcases and skeletons of hinds which he maintains were driven over by eagles. One winter day when passing up the big glen which lies at the foot of Clashven, he saw an eagle stoop at a hind and nearly knock her off the pass. Happily, after a violent struggle it regained its foot-hold or it would undoubtedly have been dashed to pieces on the rocks beneath.

He also writes, 'I am told there is a similar spot on the Reay forest where hinds are annually killed by eagles.'

Yet it is hard to find a reliable eyewitness who has actually seen a deer so panicked by eagles as to be driven in this manner over a cliff edge. I only know of one. An old crofter in Kintail told a friend of mine, Bobby MacLean, who was farming in Kintail, about a day in early June when the crofters were out gathering sheep on Ben Attow. Across the narrow gash which is Glen Lichd lies the steep green face and coires of the Five Sisters of Kintail which one sees clearly from Ben Attow. During the day, as the crofters were coming slowly along, gathering sheep ahead of them high up on the slopes of Ben Attow, they noticed deer racing wildly about on the green face of the Sisters almost opposite them. Puzzled, they halted for a rest, and a spy-glass or two was focused on the deer. They saw then that it was a small group of staggies (young stags) which were being stampeded by a pair of eagles. As they watched, it became apparent that the eagles were striving to isolate a small and weak-looking staggie from the group, one, then the other, sweeping in and with their huge wings almost buffeting the animal's head. The staggie was already tiring and lagging behind the group. Successful in isolating it the eagles then concentrated on this weakening, terror-stricken beast, while the others vanished around a ridge. They chivvied and literally herded the doomed staggie, alternately swooping to one side and the other, steering him to the precipitous edge of a steep rocky gully which sliced deep into the face of the coire. The crofters saw the staggie go over the edge, falling to his death on the rocks below.

Most of the evidence of this method of securing food remains circumstantial, however, in that below certain rock-faces deer carcases may be regularly found. If eagles are present in the area they will undoubtedly feed on this store of venison and, at some time or another, will be seen to do so. But this does not mean that the eagle was instrumental in driving them over to their deaths. I myself know of precipitous rock-faces in the Torridon area which have extremely narrow deer paths, in regular use, that I would not dare to take. Deer in steep ground seem to acquire something of the abilities of chamois, but inevitably they are subject to accidents. A falling rock, a sudden fierce gust of wind, an iced-over bit of the rock surface, all these may cause disaster and the more deer that use such paths the more likelihood of such accidents occurring. In July 1974 I found a hind lying dead below a cliff in a huge rocky coire of Ben Alligin, in Ross-shire. She was below a high, sheer rock-face which I knew was regularly traversed by the deer in that area, by way of an extremely narrow track. Practically every bone in her body was broken and her skull was crushed; her death had been immediate. She had been dead at least a week and nothing as yet had touched the carcase. A week later I passed the spot again and found that a considerable amount of now exceedingly high venison had been eaten from the carcase, while nearby, a small breast feather of an eagle, caught on a tuft of heather, pointed to at least one of the feasters. That particular coire had a pair of resident eagles and, moreover, on the lower part of the cliff, directly above the dead hind, there was a regularly-used perching ledge.

It is easy to visualise an eagle panicking the hind into her fatal slip, on a track where even one false step would be irretrievable. It is equally easy to visualise a purely accidental slip. You must decide for yourself on this subject of possible eagle predation on adult deer. I would say only this, that I believe it is definitely within the power of an eagle to succeed in such tactics, and once having tasted success, to adopt them wherever food cannot be secured more easily. Yet relatively speaking there can be few places in the Highlands which meet all the requirements – suitable situation, suitable numbers of deer and sufficient acumen on the part of an eagle – to render such predation on adult deer really significant. The description of the ruthless eagle driving the harried deer over a precipice to its death makes an infinitely better story, and appeals much more to the human craving for sensation, than that of the other version – accidental death by a fatal slip on a dangerous track. The latter is not sensational enough nor is the subsequent eating of the carrion by eagles or fox of sufficient human interest. So the legend may be more readily perpetuated than the actuality.

A factor which has figured very largely in the persecution of eagles in the past, and indeed still figures, is the accusation commonly levelled at it as a killer of lambs. As with deer calves I have no doubt that an eagle can kill a lamb. I have never witnessed it and it is difficult to get first-hand eyewitness records of the actual killing, though records of lamb remains at eyries are common-place enough. The mere presence of any trace of lamb at an eyrie is all too often taken as proof that the eagle has killed it. More often than not, I believe, lamb at an eyrie has been taken in as carrion, for there is a very appreciable death toll in lambs of the hill sheep flocks in the Highlands each lambing season. No predator will refuse such an easy source of food in favour of the more difficult killing of live prey. The only predator to hunt prey for the love of hunting is man. A predator hunts to live and the easier it is to secure the food the better, thus enabling it to conserve valuable energy in the ceaseless task of feeding itself and, at the breeding time, its young, and hence surviving as an individual and as a species. Man can afford to be more prodigal with his energies since nowadays, in this country, we need no longer struggle for the luxury of a full stomach.

In many years spent in deer, eagle and hill sheep country in the Highlands I have heard only one first-hand eyewitness account of a lamb carried off by an eagle. This was from a stalker's wife who actually witnessed it from the window of her house, high in the hills of Perthshire. In the absence of her husband she saw an eagle stoop from the sky at a small weakly lamb and carry it off, despite her screams of abuse as she rushed out of the door, too late to prevent the tiny tragedy. In my own personal experience based on regular visits to eyries right in the middle of hill sheep ground, lambs did not figure largely at eyries, neither in any one year nor over the period of twenty years. I began watching eagles in 1957 and it was 1963 before I saw lamb at an eyrie. There is certainly little justification for the often almost hysterical hatred of eagles as a species still prevalent here and there because of its ill-fame as a lamb-killer. One can readily understand any shepherd who cares for his sheep being unable to relish the sight of lamb at an eyrie. I find it hard to avoid being partisan when I see the remains of a dappled deer calf at an eyrie. There are however many more young lambs, and deer calves, lost each year through natural causes and accidental deaths than are lost to the eagle. Making a comparison of the population figures in the Highlands of upwards of 200,000 red deer, more than 2,000,000 hill sheep, and only 250–300 pairs of golden eagles, should lead to some sense of proportion on this issue. As a final word on the number of lambs I have recorded at my eyries over a 20-year period: they have occurred less frequently than deer calf, and I have never recorded more than the remains of five deer calves at any one eyrie in a nesting season.

If I may sum up then, while I know the eagle to be powerful enough to kill both red deer calf and lamb, I believe it more often profits by those found dead, in both species, than by actual kills made.

In areas where wild goats (that is, feral goats) co-exist with eagles there is undoubtedly some predation on the young, but the remarks regarding deer calves and lambs also apply to wild goats, especially perhaps as the kids of these wild goats are born at possibly the most inhospitable time of the year in the Highlands, late January and early February. I once found a very recently-killed and part-eaten wild goat kid, only a day or so old, while on the island of Mull in early February

1974. The tiny black-and-white-coated carcase weighed a scant 5 lb and bore the unmistakable talon punctures of an eagle. My study area not being in wild goat country I have never recorded remains at an eyrie, but such remains have been recorded at eyries in the Highlands. I have not as yet recorded roe deer remains at an eyrie either, though I did once come upon the carcase of a dead yearling roe on which an eagle had been feeding. As the living animal could not have weighed any more than an October red deer calf it is not beyond probability that it had been a kill. On the other hand, as it was early Spring, the season of natural mortality, the likelihood is that it was a weakling which had already died. Reports of roe fawns being taken in as prey have occasionally been made and as a recently-born roe fawn only scales 4–5 lb it would not be difficult for an eagle to carry one into its eyrie. They would be less vulnerable than red deer calves however in that they would rarely be found outside the cover of woodlands.

I well remember my first experience of seeing fox as prey, in 1960, at an eyrie of pair B, from which in due course two young survived to fly. The remains were the hind-quarters and tail of an adult fox, not a fox cub. Since then I have seen fox often enough to make me almost blasé. Certainly often enough to balance out the number of times lamb remains have been seen, let alone the percentage of those which may have been kills. In most cases when fox was recorded it was in the form of fox cubs. Fox cubs, who live in high-ground dens of rocky cairns or dry peat holes, can be very vulnerable to the keen eyes and silent glide of the eagle when they are at play, as they get older, outside their dens. Having had success once at a particular den, I believe an eagle is likely to keep an eye on it in the future. At an eyrie of pair A, in 1961, I found fox cub as prey on three separate visits, all of which I judged had been taken from the same den. In 1975 at an eyrie of pair C I found fox cub on two separate visits, and again I thought they were

Eaglets – 6 weeks old – at an eyrie

White down on the head of a 6-week-old eaglet

At 9 weeks the golden-brown feathers have come through

from the same den, though a period of around four weeks separated the two occurrences.

In the cases where I found adult fox at eyries these could well have been picked up as dead by the eagles. There is an unrelenting warfare throughout the Highlands against the fox and has been for generations, without it significantly diminishing their numbers, and seldom is a fox that is killed by stalker or shepherd buried afterwards. Having first made this point I am also quite sure than an eagle is fully capable of killing a fox if it succeeds in taking it completely unawares, and sinks its lethal talons into the spine before the fox can take evasive or defensive measures.

It would seem that eagles may make a combined attack on an adult fox for Tom Speedy in his book *The Natural History of Scotland with Rod and Gun* refers to an eyewitness account of this:

On one occasion when hind-shooting in company with Campbell, the keeper, and when climbing the west end of Cruchan mountain in Ross-shire, our attention was attracted by two eagles behaving in a peculiar and excitable manner. Sitting down, and with the aid of our glasses, we discovered the object of their fury and excitement. These savage birds had espied a fox on the open green slope of the mountain side where there was no cover of any sort but where it was doing its best to reach a place of concealment. Unfortunately for him a third eagle joined in the fray and the fight grew fast and furious. Reynard had to fight for his life, and he did this by snapping at them, running when he could and at times squatting on the ground. He was however quickly roused to activity by a daring swoop by the savage birds almost striking him with their wings. The eagles were evidently aware of his dangerous jaws and were intent on harassing him till an opportunity presented itself when they could clutch him with their talons. He would at times make off as fast as he could but only to be pulled up again in a daring swoop by one and sometimes two of the eagles. He now got into a hollow in the ground where we could not see him but where the powerful birds kept swooping over him and it appeared as if they could not strike to the same advantage as on the level. Two of the eagles now settled on the ground close together, their golden hackles standing erect, which made them resemble two old wives hobnobbing, with shawls over their heads. The third bird kept on the wing, making an occasional swoop over the fox but evidently to no purpose, as he did not seem to move, and it also sat down. We were on the point of leaving when we again saw two of the eagles on the move. The fox had thought the coast was clear, and made rapidly for a cairn of stones some distance off. It appeared as if the royal birds were aware of this as they were now more daring than ever and did not want to be done out of their dinner. They swooped continually sometimes knocking him aside and over. His springs and snaps at them were much less frequent but every chance he had he tried to make for the cairn. His next and most feeble move was over the ridge and out of our sight but we could plainly see he was about to give up. For a few minutes, we could see the eagles rise above the ridge and swoop down again, doubtless still harassing their victim and when they finally disappeared we concluded the doom of Reynard was sealed. Anxious to know the fate of Reynard we ascended to the place the following morning and found patches of fur along where the fight had taken place. Further on over the ridge we discovered, with the aid of a retriever, the entrails of the fox, which was proof positive that they had killed and devoured him, and carried off what was left of his remains.

The presence of three eagles at that time was probably composed of two parent adult birds and their apprentice young one of that year, still learning his trade. Another revealing account of the way of an eagle with an adult fox is related by H. Mortimer Batten in his *British Wild Animals*:

The golden eagle is probably the only one who takes regular toll of the moorland foxes. They not uncommonly lift cubs and carry them to their eyries and Donald Stewart told me of an eagle's attack upon an adult fox, which he witnessed. When he arrived at the scene the fox was standing close under an isolated boulder and the eagle was perched on top of it. The fox stood with his brush held rigidly vertical, ready to serve as a foil, and every time the eagle struck at him he dodged around the rock at lightning speed. He was however a very frightened fox knowing that if once these terrible talons closed upon him his doom was sealed. The eagle was clearly trying to scare him from his retreat but the fox had more sense than to make a dash across the open for the certain cover of some rocks fifty yards away. The eagle would have caught him long before he got there so he continued to dodge round and round his solitary boulder, keeping so closely under it that the great bird could not get a clear whack at him.

Stalemate! but a very frightened fox.

Gordon Addison, one-time colleague of mine and an experienced and hardy stalker, witnessed an eagle's attack on an adult fox which was inspired by a more selfless motive than a desire for food. It happened on Braeroy, Inverness-shire, in May 1966, while he was out on the hill with gun and terrier looking for signs of foxes. An eagle persistently swooping at something among some heather knolls and peat hags attracted his attention but he was quite close before he saw that the object of the eagle's attack was a big fox. So preoccupied were eagle and fox that he managed to get a long shot at the fox but without apparent success. The fox bolted and at once Gordon's red-coated Border terrier ran forward in pursuit. To Gordon's utter consternation the eagle immediately transferred its attention to the running, sandy-red terrier and swooping from the rear, had it up in the air in a trice, dangling, struggling, from its talons. Gordon, dumbfounded, recovered his wits in time to fire the shot from his remaining barrel into the air above the eagle which at once released its grip on the terrier, and it fell to the heather. It was stunned by the impact and had nasty talon marks on its body, but, a wiry, hardy wee beastie, it eventually recovered. After attending to his terrier, Gordon cast around to see if perhaps his shot had hit the fox and it was then that he found, close by, but out of sight at first in the peat hags, a second eagle, standing grounded, with a rabbit-sized gin trap on one enormous foot. The sudden appearance of Gordon apparently vitalised the eagle into a supreme effort and it took wing, the trap dangling, leaving, where it had been, remains of prey which its mate must have been regularly bringing to it. To me this whole episode is a striking instance of the devotion of an eagle to its handicapped mate: in attacking the fox which obviously had harboured designs on the grounded bird, then in attacking the terrier, apparently a fresh danger to its mate, and not least in regularly taking prey to the trapped bird.

Gordon never saw a trace of the eagle with the dangling trap again. It may have eventually succeeded in getting rid of the trap, at the expense of a talon perhaps. I hope so.

I have heard, at first hand, of other instances of an eagle attacking a terrier and in these cases too I imagine the eagle associated the terrier with fox, with whom they seem to be at constant enmity.

Another former colleague and friend of mine, the late John MacDonald,

Red deer hind and calf

Grouse occur frequently as prey at an eyrie –

as well as the stoat and his victim, the rabbit.

Fox, part eaten, at an eyrie

Eaglet feeding on the hind-quarters of a red deer calf

more familiarly known to all in Fort Augustus as 'Johnny Kytra', told me of finding wild cat kittens as prey on an occupied eyrie. Another friend was once lucky enough, while out hind-stalking, to watch an eagle stoop repeatedly at a wild cat in the hills above Stratherrick, in Inverness-shire. He had a particularly good view of this because the wild cat was outlined against a large drift of frozen snow, as it rose up from time to time on its hind-legs to swipe at the attacking eagle, which eventually desisted and went in search of easier prey.

A less prudent eagle met with partial success but in so doing sowed the seeds of its own destruction, as described in Bannerman's *The Birds of the British Isles* Vol. 10:

The encounter took place near Mam Ratagan, in Kintail, in January 1909 when Sir Philip Christison and a shepherd named John MacRae saw through their glasses a wild cat making a meal of a white hare. There was frozen snow on the hill at the time. Suddenly an eagle swooped down several times, and alighted a few yards from the cat. It then sidled up to it and the cat went for it. A struggle ensued and the eagle raised flight by hopping to the edge of a small cliff, with the cat hanging on. The eagle flattened out, then began to gain height. When very high – Sir Philip estimated 1500–2000 feet above the hill – he and his companion saw the cat coming down and found it dashed to pieces on the rocks. Next day word that a sick eagle had been seen about three miles away brought them to the scene where a golden eagle, terribly wounded inside the thighs and unable to move, was found. The bird was put out of its misery and was eventually presented to the Royal Scottish Museum.

An anecdote with a touch of humour, or poetic justice if you like, was told to me some years ago by a veteran crofter-fisherman from Diabaig, Wester Ross. Years later I read the same story in the reprinted issue of *Gairloch* by J. H. Dixon, first published in 1886. From it I quote:

The next anecdote is of an eagle near Kinlochewe. This injudicious bird carried off a cat to feed its two young at its eyrie – probably on Meall a' Ghuibhais. The cat was still alive and well when deposited on the eagle's nest. Pussy made short work of the two eaglets and returned home safe and sound. This incident is traditional, not only to Gairloch, but also in the neighbouring territory. I understand that in Assynt and Kintail, as well as in Gairloch, the following Gaelic riddle is often asked, the answer being this very anecdote. Here is a literal English translation: 'Some food went to two at the head of Loch Maree; the food ate the two, and the food came home again?'

This incident could have actually occurred. A cat carried in, stunned or shocked, by the male eagle and simply dumped on the eyrie, with its two helpless young eaglets; the male, typically, flying off at once; the cat, reviving before the absent female arrived to tear up any prey to feed the young with, itself eating the young, and departing. It makes a good story, with the added merit of being just possible.

The same veteran from Diabaig told me that he knew of occasions when an eagle had swooped on one of the large coalfish which, long years ago, often swam near the surface of Loch Torridon. A very large coalfish was once found dead, washed ashore, with an eagle attached to it, talons still fast-imbedded in its flesh. It was supposed that the eagle had tackled too large and strong a fish, which, on being struck had dived and so drowned the eagle, then died itself. The eagle in this case could have been a sea eagle, a species which would still have been present in my informant's younger days.

The Prey of Eagles

James Conway in his *Forays Among Salmon and Deer* refers to an encounter between eagle and otter:

On one occasion an eagle was seen struggling violently with some other animal on the surface of a pool. Donald's father chanced to be near with a gun and thinking that he might possibly get a salmon for supper he shot the eagle and at the same time, to his surprise, he killed a large otter, the eagle's talons so deeply imbedded in its back that the two could not be separated.

Here again, I imagine, this eagle could have been a sea eagle. It must be a very rare occurrence for an eagle to tangle with an otter. Instances are also on record of eagles swooping at salmon or sea trout; eagles, I hasten to add, not ospreys.

H. Mortimer Batten, in his *British Wild Animals* already referred to, writes of an attack on a pine marten by an eagle:

As a boy he one day saw an eagle perched on a rock watching for young rabbits to appear from the screes below. Something moved among the screes and the eagle instantly spread its wings and swooped. The movement however was not that of rabbit but of a pine marten, there for the same purpose as the eagle. The result was that there was the dickens of an explosion when they met. The marten flew at the eagle and the feathers also flew. The eagle 'screamed' and dropped to earth, sitting back on its fanned-out tail, talons presented (typical defensive posture of a grounded eagle), but by that time the pine marten was back among the rocks and did not reappear.

I have myself recorded a much smaller predator at an eyrie of pair B in 1960, a stoat, and this has also been recorded by other observers. The capture of such a small, hardy, quicksilver animal is indeed tribute to both the speed and skill of the eagle's silent approach, though stoat must surely make a tough, rank meal even for an omnivorous young eagle.

Most of these incidents narrated above, authentic as I believe them to be, must be of relatively rare occurrence, recorded as they are from sources going back over a hundred years. The main livelihood of eagles, is, I am sure, derived from more normal prey: hare, rabbit, grouse, ptarmigan and carrion.

Probably the most sensational of the alleged depredations of the eagle is that on human babies. As long ago as 1701 the Rev. J. Brand in *A brief description of Orkney etc, 1701*, refers to a child being carried by an eagle from Orphir to Hoy in the Orkneys. Charles St John in his *Sport and Natural History in Morayshire*, 1863, writes: 'I have heard frequent stories of a child being carried away by an eagle but could never trace these home to their source.' In my own native village there was a man whose byname was Donnelly Eagle. This man was said to have been lifted by an eagle, whilst a very young baby, and fortunately dropped without injury. The story, as told to me, was that the family, including the mother (as was common enough in those days in crofting families), was at work making hay on an upland field. The baby, wrapped in a white shawl, was left lying comfortably asleep in the shade of a coil of hay. An eagle swooped and lifted the tiny infant, but luckily the shawl came loose and the sleeping child tumbled out when hardly clear of the ground. A unique distinction for the child to have 'eagle' affixed to him for life as a sobriquet.

I realised only a year or two ago just how easily these legends continue to flourish, when a summer visitor to Torridon, in talking of the single pair of eagles then nesting in the Lake District of England, assured

Golden eagle in flight

Twin roe deer fawns – an unusual sight

Young vixen

me that during an evening's pub session there a local farmer had solemnly told him that one of these eagles had attempted unsuccessfully to carry off a 2-year-old child, leaving talon marks on the child's neck. This was undoubtedly a 'tall one' on the part of the local, to an open-mouthed visitor. The danger is that the recipient implicitly believed it and recounted it as fact thereafter.

At the other end of the scale, prey so triflingly small as to seem unworthy of the notice of an eagle but which I have personally recorded at eyries over the years includes wing cases of a black beetle, an almost naked, unfledged ring ousel nestling, the empty nest of a meadow pipit which must have contained nestlings when carried in, grouse chicks so tiny as to have been only hours old, bank-vole, black water-vole and, once, a mole. I am of the opinion that the golden eagle, unlike the peregrine falcon, takes most, though not all, of its prey from the ground, including grouse and ptarmigan. It will of course at times take the latter two species in the air, both being inclined to be direct fliers which do not seem to have, or to use, any talent for jinking and dodging in flight. Charles St John, a fine field-naturalist of his day, writes:

Generally the eagle hovers nearly motionless above her prey (supposing it to be grouse or hare) at a very great height; suddenly closing her wings she drops as if to fall to the ground but, stopping her course at the height of perhaps forty or fifty feet, she again hovers motionless for a short time, then she drops with great rapidity on the unfortunate animal and if it is small enough lifts it at once from the ground and carries it away. At an animal flying or running she makes a great dash, appears to surround it with her wings and seldom fails to catch it.

Yet Tom Wallace, a very good and observant friend of mine and a welcome ally on many an expedition into the hill, saw different tactics employed by an eagle, unsuccessfully one must admit, but only just. Out on the heather flank of a hill south-east of Inverness he heard a noise which he could only liken to the acceleration of a jet plane which has just torn the Highland stillness to shreds. Turning sharply he saw that it was caused by the rush of air through the stiffly-held wings of a golden eagle, pursuing, in an incredibly fast glide, a grouse, whose short wings far from being held motionless were beating the air in a blur of rapid strokes. The grouse, only a few yards ahead of the eagle when Tom saw it, just managed to attain the cover of the heather and rock-clad hillside, in a split-second escape from the hurtling death behind. The disappointed eagle pulled out of its swoop only inches above the hillside, it seemed. Had it hit the hill at that speed it would have meant injury, or death.

I think most readers will agree from the foregoing that the eagle's tastes in prey are widespread indeed, and worthy of still further study. A list of different prey recorded at eyries of my study pairs of eagles during the twenty years of observation is given in the Appendix at the end of this work.

PART IV

Observation Diary

I began my study of the golden eagle, as I have said, in 1957, first with pair A, and, subsequently, enlarged it to include another three pairs, B, C and D. In the years 1957 to 1969 I pursued this study from Fort Augustus, at first using a bicycle for the miles of road I had to cover before I could take to the hill, and later, with greater ease, using a motorbike. In July 1969 I moved to a position with the National Trust for Scotland at Torridon, Wester Ross, but even from its remoteness I managed to continue my study. A car was necessary then and sometimes I covered more than 2000 miles in an eagle season, driving from Torridon to the Monadhliaths and back. On my many visits to eyries, from 1957 to 1976, interest was never lacking, quite apart from the fascination of watching the eaglets grow, and recording the varied items of prey which featured over the years. Going, latterly, by car from sea level at Torridon, the road wound through rugged hills and alongside long sheltered lochs. Then, on foot, I made a steep ascent to cross a difficult high-ground peaty plateau at around 2000 ft, typically Monadhliaths terrain, dotted with black lochans and seamed with deep, black peat runners. Finally, the plunge deep into the eagle glen and the arduous toil up to the eyries on the opposite side.

All this meant a wide variety of landscape and wildlife. The early morning starts, too, just after dawn throughout May, June and July, were conducive to intriguing glimpses of wild animals and birds, confident in the knowledge that most of humanity was still in bed. A roe deer, browsing fastidiously on the fresh green of the May larch needles – it is only the flash of her white rump that betrays her in the dim recesses of the aisles of young larches; two velvet-knobbed red deer stags, ponderous of gait and shabby of coat compared to the dainty, dark-coated roe, pacing, one behind the other, alongside the parallel steel lines of the Inverness to Kyle of Lochalsh railway. Undisturbed in the early morning quiet they are in no hurry, slowly leaving the glen bottoms where they have been grazing in the security of the night, for the more certain solitude of the hill where they will lie up during the day. A sight with a touch of comedy, as I passed very early one morning, was a stalker's lonely house, with a number of uninvited guests, stags no less, feeding in his garden, while he slept blissfully unaware. His spring cabbage must have had a severe setback that year.

On the roadside loch, close to which I park my car when I take to the hill, a black-throated diver, a study in quiet elegance, sits proudly erect, on her water's-edge nest, safe in the inviolability of her island site; curlews wailing in supplication on a stretch of low moorland, an anxious yet betraying pleading which bespeaks new-hatched young; a meadow pipit flutters out at my very feet, from the base of a tussock of deer grass, disclosing the neat deerhair-lined cup of her nest with its four eggs.

Higher up, golden plovers, black-bellied with gold-flecked backs, scuttle like clockwork mice from one torran* to another, incessantly voicing their disquiet. From the high plateau the distant line of often snow-clad peaks to the north-west appears on the horizon, jagged white peaks as intimidating as the Himalayas. By the edge of a hill lochan, waters still and black as a mirror of jet, I observe the secretive, crouched stillness of a red-throated diver on her nest, apprehensive

*torran: hillock or knoll.

of the presence of a passer-by. Long grey neck extended, velvet-grey head, with its unwinking ruby eyes, flat to the ground, she tries, not altogether unsuccessfully, to merge with the grey rock behind her. And always deer, mainly hinds and their calves in that particular area. Only the unmistakable indication of wariness, the wide-set ears and questing muzzle at the end of the long slender neck of a red deer hind, is visible over a low ridge, until a couple of hesitant steps bring her body into view as she strives to identify the disturber of her normally quiet hill. Well might she be anxious, for in June behind her may lie her new-born calf, a dappled youngster of never-failing delight, curled up trustingly in its nook in the heather. The safeguard of instinctive fear would come in a day or two. At the moment the deer calf trusts the whole world, a trust sadly misplaced if hungry fox or hunting eagle happens along and its mother is not at hand to defend it. More rarely, you spot the silent, furtive, yet speedy movement of a hill fox, body and bushy tail one sandy-yellow straight line – a fleeting glimpse here and there as he streaks away among the peat hags.

A ring ousel (mountain blackbird seems a much better name), flute-flute-fluting from a rocky ridge; grouse with guttural, rattling exhortation; grey-speckled ptarmigan with weird sepulchral croak; anxiously-piping greenshank, white rump twinkling as she twists and turns in agitated flight – all, at one time or another, enlivened the way to the eyries. Throughout the summer snipe, sandpiper, dipper and grey wagtail are seen and heard in the eyrie glen. Little wonder the lure of it was so strong even if one also had to accept the bad days when the weather was so foul and the hill so inhospitable that it appeared lifeless except for the striving figure of the eagle-watcher.

The varied wild flowers which even the bleakest parts of the Highlands can support, especially in late May and June, also added their attraction to the eagle trips. At road level carpets of wild thyme looked and smelt delightful, the profuse diminutive white stars of heath bed-straw mingling with them. About the loch's edge, pinky-white spikes of bog bean rose from the dark water. A little above road level the damp flats were sprinkled with the short spires of spotted orchids. A little further and the dainty, white, ethereal-looking flowers of wood sorrel, backed by their equally delicate pale green leaves, lined the path. Higher up, the broad green leaves of lady's mantle appeared long before the pale yellow flower came, often sprinkled with tiny jewels of moisture, to be displaced, higher still, by the smaller leafage of alpine lady's mantle. As the path wound higher little clumps of yellow mountain saxifrage appeared. At the top, among stunted blaeberry and the sparse heathers and lichens of the high-ground plateau, dwarf birch (*betula nana*) wound its secretive, small-leafed tendrils, relic of a much colder era and, significantly, still able to survive on that cold upland. Here too the immaculate, white, paper-like single flowers of cloudberry enlivened, briefly, the monotones of dark greens, browns and greys. Tucked away here and there, the white flowers of dwarf cornel, with their distinctive black central disc, disclosed themselves. On the harder green slopes of the eagle glen, yellow tormentil and deep blue milkwort sprinkled the green, and on the damp green ledge directly below the eyrie the delicate white stars of the aptly-named starry saxifrage gleamed.

Some seasons were, inevitably, more full of interest than others and I give an account here of my detailed observations of pair C, in four different years, on two eyries (E2 and E5) which were the favourites of the six sites available to this pair.

Though I began eagle-watching in 1957 it was not until 1963 that I was lucky enough to be present when an eagle's egg was hatching and so was able to establish the exact age of the young in that eyrie and keep a record, week by week, until the young left the eyrie, fully fledged.

It was not until 1974 that a similar opportunity arose and, even better, it was in the same glen, and at the same eyrie as in 1963, so that conditions were ideal for comparing the two seasons, 1963 and 1974.

When I did the 1963 study I was still living at Culachy, near Fort Augustus, right in my study area, as it were. I had no car at that time and to visit this eyrie I first had to cycle eight strenuous miles, then leave my bike and walk for two hours through the hill to my eyrie, reversing the performance on the way back.

1963

APRIL 20TH

A dry, clear day as I checked up on pair C's eyries. I found the female sitting on the third eyrie I went to. I saw the pale gold top of her head first, as she sat low in the centre of the wide nest. She rose to her feet unhurriedly, indeed with dignity, took a step to the edge of the nest and threw herself off, flying at no great height over my head and away parallel to the green hill-face. Turning, while still in my view, she seemed to debate whether to fly back over me again, but thought better of it and soared out high over the glen, ultimately going out of sight. This nest was readily accessible, a wide nest under a fairly deep overhang, built on a long ledge covered with moss and wood-rush. It was not very high; the cavity was lined with great wood-rush with a couple of tufts of common rush and of crowberry mixed in with this. Two large eggs formed the clutch, smooth-looking and almost colour-less, a dingy white with a scarcely perceptible greenish tinge and with one or two faintly limned rusty streaks as if washed on with a brushful of very weak water-colour.

MAY 4TH

A nasty afternoon of continual cold rain driving in before a southerly wind. The female was incubating, sitting tight, head pointing in towards the rock-face, and on the exposed outer edge of the nest bits of wood-rush moved in the wind. When she took wing I found the two eggs still unhatched but then, as I stood there, I heard, without realising what it was, a distinct cheeping which seemed to be coming from the nest. One of the eggs was actually hatching and through the small jagged-edged hole in the thick shell I could dimly see the dark beak of the cheeping eaglet, waggling weakly about. I left quickly so that the female could resume her duties, noticing the naked hinder end of a grouse, lying as prey on the edge of the nest. On my way back, above a longish loch near where I'd left my bike, I heard the wailing cry of a black-throated diver and then saw a pair floating at the far end of the loch. As I watched, one half rolled and momentarily displayed dazzling white underparts. A few deer were making their way in to the birches which clad the face here, seeking shelter from the inclement weather. My own fingers were so cold I could hardly press my camera's release button.

MAY 11TH

A better day, still coldish but, blessedly dry. The female was again on the nest and flew off when I was only yards from it. Both eggs had now hatched. The eaglets were small and clad entirely in white down; one was only half the size of its nestmate. I was dubious of its chances of survival if food should be scarce and its larger nestmate aggressive. A recently-hatched eaglet is a puny little object, no larger than an adult sparrow and weighing a scant 2 oz but it is incredibly fast-growing and the larger eaglet, at a week old, already weighed 1 lb and the smaller one 8 oz. I weighed them by means of a small spring balance and a plastic bag, or rather a series of plastic bags increasing in size and strength as the eaglets did. In the early stages it was easy to put the tiny eaglet into the bag and suspend this from the balance but in the last few weeks it became a trial of strength and patience on my part.

Both eaglets were very lethargic, typical of young birds of prey, their awkwardly sprawled-out bodies jerking a little to the tune of their faint incessant cheeping. The smaller eaglet was more awake than the larger one, perhaps not as fully fed. No sign of fresh greenery on the nest which still retained its shallow central cup. Again, the hinder end of a plucked grouse lay on an edge. Built as it is, on a long ledge which communicates with the hill-face, this is the only eyrie I know in which the young, at a more active stage, would be able to actually walk right off the nest, on to the hill-face.

The parents were in the air as I left the eyrie, one (the male?) considerably higher than the other.

MAY 18TH

A vile day, after a night of ceaseless rain which had made every burn high, and difficult to cross, and all the hill waterfalls tumultuous and white. There was fresh snow on the tops and a positive blizzard of wet snow swept down on me as I was crossing the high peat hag top. The female came off when I was still a hundred yards from the eyrie; she could not have been brooding long as both eaglets looked distinctly damp. The remains of three grouse lay on the nest, two of the pieces half under the sleeping eaglets. They had visibly grown in one week and the disparity in size continued to be marked. It was obvious in weight also, the larger was now almost 2 lb and the smaller 1 lb. The eyrie has still had no fresh green leafage at it this year, though today a damp straggle of greeny-yellow sphagnum moss lay on it. On my way back the female accompanied me until I began to cross the high plateau, gliding above, three times alighting on the ridge ahead of me, then taking wing as I drew near. Once, sky-lined on the ridge, she shook out her feathers in irritable fashion, as if dispelling moisture from them.

MAY 25TH

A black-throated diver was floating serenely out on a roadside loch, trying to ignore the presence of a rowing boat from which two anglers were hopefully casting. A few deer, untidy in faded sandy-yellow coats, were feeding high on the first face as I climbed it, after leaving my bike hidden as usual. For the first time this year there were sheep and lambs in the eagles' glen – and for the first time since I began watching eagles in 1957 I saw lamb as prey on an eyrie – the body of a very tiny, obviously prematurely-born lamb, weighing only 2 lb, and the leg of a larger lamb. The female was absent when I arrived and I could distinctly hear one of the eaglets cheeping as I came in below the nest. Both eaglets were awake and still entirely white, down-clad, but, again, noticeably larger. They were twice as heavy as at the previous weighing. My spring balance registered just below 4 lb for the larger and just 2 lb for the smaller. The smaller one kept up a continual cheeping (hungry?), but the larger one lay quite silent. Besides the lamb there was a scattering of black water-vole fur on the nest, near a fresh green sprig of crowberry. The female was keeping an eye on me from the air, above the eyrie cliff, and after I'd left the nest and was about halfway up the face on the opposite side I became aware of her above me. So she was going to convoy me out of her glen again. She landed on the ridge above, to fly again and then to alight, this time on a small straggly rowan tree which seemed inadequate for her bulk. Once more she took leave of me as I crested the ridge, judging me safely away from her eyrie now. On my final descent to where I'd left my bike I heard the excited croaking of hooded crows and eventually tracked it to high in the sky where two eagles were gliding, a considerable distance apart, each being attacked by a hoodie. The hoodies were so close that they seemed to be almost alighting on the eagles' backs. The eagles made no attempt at retaliation but eventually one, then the other, went into a fast glide eastwards, leaving their tormentors far behind. This was the territory of pair B, who also were rearing young that year.

JUNE IST

A glorious day, sunny and warm; it was good to be alive and walking the hill. As I crossed the high-ground plateau I saw a hind, her coat all spiked with wet black peat, emerge from a hollow ahead where she'd been cooling herself with a peat bath. She joined another hind a little further on who had also been indulging in a peat wallow. Their black, faintly glistening coats gave them an almost pre-historic aspect, slightly awesome to the imaginative. Most of the deer I saw were lying on moist peat banks in an attempt to keep cool. As I finally neared the eyrie I could again hear the cheeping of an eaglet, probably the younger one, less well fed than its stronger nestmate and thus inclined to keep fretfully appealing for food. At the eyrie I was very surprised to see both eaglets out of the actual nest, lying apart from each other on the green ledge to one side of the nest. At 4 weeks old the larger now weighed $5\frac{1}{4}$ lb, an increase of $1\frac{1}{4}$ lb, but the smaller, at $2\frac{1}{2}$ lb had only gained $\frac{1}{2}$ lb. Dottings of black, the first indication of feathering, were just beginning to be apparent on wing edges. The nest was now a flattened platform, all trace of central hollow gone, but it was still not too tattered or withered looking. No prey at all on the nest, yet there were plenty of lambs to be had in the glen if the eagle so desired. I was again halfway up the face on my return journey when I became aware of the female on patrol above – my last sight of her being a 'falling stone' display as she quickly lost height.

JUNE 8TH

An even hotter day than my last visit. The deer were all lying among the peat banks, or in the deep shade of rock-faces. Yet again I could hear the cheeping of the smaller eaglet as I drew near the nest. When I reached it the larger one was on the nest, the smaller on the ledge to one side. The remains of a plucked grouse, and a bank-vole, very small prey indeed, lay on the nest. The larger eaglet was assuming a dark-speckled appearance now, though still predominately white, and it weighed 7 lb, the smaller only 4 lb, an increase of 1¾ and 1½ lb respectively. For the first time, fresh green leafage was apparent on the nest, flowered sprays of rowan leaves and a tuft of green heather. One of the adult eagles, the female I suspect, was patrolling above the ridge as I left the eyrie, body and wings looking almost black, while the head appeared almost white, in striking contrast.

As I came back over the top I nearly trod on a dozing hind lying close into a small rock-face – she was startled into frantic activity. The hill was now a mass of small flowers, starry saxifrage, milkwort, cloudberry, dwarf cornel, mountain everlasting and tormentil, with spotted orchids brightening the lower and greener slopes.

JUNE 15TH

I watched nine hinds file over the ridge ahead of me and noted one miniature, daintily dappled calf valiantly trotting with them. As I approached the eyrie the female eagle appeared and landed about 400 yards above the eyrie. She was on the wing again when I reached the eyrie but then returned and sat broodingly above. Watching me? As usual an eaglet was cheeping as I drew near and, unseen, I came in this time above the nest. Peering over I saw the larger bird standing erect on the nest while the smaller, cheeping in frustration, was standing by a grouse carcase and ineffectually trying to pick bits from it. The larger, at 6 weeks old, now weighed 8 lb 6 oz, the smaller, 5 lb, an increase of 1 lb 6 oz, and 1 lb respectively over last week. On the nest were the carcases of two grouse, one plucked, one only partly plucked. There was also a small pinkish foot, of either immature ring ousel or meadow pipit; small prey, barely a beakful for the young eaglets now. A few sprays of fading rowan leaves lay on the nest and by the scatterings of feathers and the flattening of vegetation it appears that the whole ledge as well as the wide nest is being regularly used by the eaglets. The female joined me as I was halfway up the opposite face and alighted quite close on the ridge above me. She left, and landing on a cliff-face on the eyrie side of the glen she disappeared at once, merging into its background. No wonder eagles are so seldom seen, except when airborne, if they can merge into a rock landscape thus. I was nearly at the top when she appeared again, approaching me now head on, low, almost on a level with me, giving me a magnificent view of her light yellow-gold head and awe-inspiring wing-span. A grouse rose below her and set off westwards at high speed but she paid no heed. Perhaps she only had eyes for me at that stage until I was safely away from her territory once more.

JUNE 22ND

A weeping, grey, unattractive start to the day as I left, about 5 a.m., to cycle the first stretch of my weekly pilgrimage. This time, before I was halfway down the face into the eagle glen, the female appeared above, and quite low too, her head looking very light-coloured, whitish in fact. I kept on, conscious that she was in the air above me, but not really giving her much thought. A moment later I heard that nerve-wracking, tearing swoosh, which I had become familiar with at an eyrie of pair A in 1959. By the time I looked up after my involuntary jump she was already high above, but I must admit I kept one respectful eye on her from then on, the back of my neck feeling singularly bare and exposed. The nest was still a good half-mile away when I heard the familiar cheeping of the smaller eaglet and when I got to it, it was to see that this eaglet was looking distinctly seedy in comparison to the obviously thriving larger one. It was not nearly so far advanced in feathering and even though traces of blood about its beak testified to a recent meal, it had lost $\frac{1}{2}$ lb in the week's interval since my previous visit. The larger eaglet had only gained 1 oz, it was now 8 lb 7 oz. We had had a week of rainy, misty weather, of depressing, grey visibility. Had this bad visibility contributed to a scarcity of prey brought in to the eyrie? It certainly appeared so. The remains of a couple of grouse lay on the nest; the trampled platform was now distinctly unattractive, dirty-brown with no greenery in evidence at all. Leaving the eyrie some time later I was below it and out of sight of the eaglets when a sudden clamorous outburst of cheeping, from both eaglets, caused me to look up and I saw the female sweep low over the eyrie, head bent as if scanning it to make sure I had done no damage. She ignored the hungry appeals of her young and swept away, majestically, along the face, appearing as usual to convoy me on my way when I was at the halfway stage up the opposite face.

It seems clear to me that the male is still doing the bulk of the hunting while the female is always on guard near the eyrie. In this respect she is the most obviously watchful female eagle I have so far encountered. Moreover she seems to be becoming bolder, perhaps getting used to my appearances at her eyrie, and she looks impressively menacing in her approach at times, a straight black bar, gliding with rigid wings, her light-coloured head driving, arrow-straight, on a level with my head, pulling up long before she reaches me.

Coming over the ridge I found myself almost on top of three hinds and a new calf. The hinds ran at once, the calf ran also, but only for a few yards before it folded up in a dry peat hag. Approaching cautiously, camera ready, I saw that its head was up, alert, but as I came into view it gradually sank until it was lying stretched out along the peaty apron. One hind-leg was still stuck out, ridiculously, rigidly behind, as if it had not had time to pull it in comfortably below its body. Its dappled flanks were heaving uncontrollably, engendering a positive feeling of shame in me, for myself and for all humans, that we could be the cause of such instinctive fear in one so young and helpless. I took a photograph and, as I suspected might happen, the click of the camera shutter seemed to break the spell which had kept the calf immobile. Infinitely slowly and, it seemed, reluctantly the dark head came up, liquid eyes framed in gracefully curved long eyelashes, ears wide-spread. With an apprehensive look in my direction the calf rose and made a tottering move away from me, gaining more control over its wavering legs as it got under way but it was still distinctly wobbly as it disappeared. Easy prey for fox or eagle if it had run thus in their sight, I thought, as I moved off again.

JUNE 29TH
A dreadful day with clinging grey mist low on the hill, hiding all the tops. All the burns too were high, and difficult to cross. I had some trouble in finding the eyrie in the mist which shrouded the face and it was the audible cheeping of an eaglet which eventually guided me

to it. On the withered platform of the nest the larger eaglet was standing, damp and rather dejected looking, over the complete skeleton of a deer calf, every vestige of flesh cleaned off it. The memory of my encounter last week with the charmingly-alive deer calf was so vivid that I hated to see this evidence of such dainty creatures providing food for the eagle at times. With a stirring of foreboding I looked for the smaller eaglet, and saw it lying sprawled out, dead, on a green ledge directly below the nest. It must have died shortly after my last visit for its feathering was no more advanced. I examined it, but there was no appearance of it having been actively ill-treated or killed by the larger one. It had simply died of slow starvation, denied the share of the food it needed by the stronger, first-hatched eaglet. It seemed significant that it had died at around 7 weeks old, just when the eaglets reach the stage of being able to deal with the prey by themselves. While the female had been tearing the prey up and actually feeding both young the weaker had been getting just enough to keep it alive. When it had had to compete directly with the larger eaglet for a share of the prey brought in, it had not, at a stage when prey may well have been scarce, been able to survive. If prey had been plentiful I have no doubt the balance would have been tipped in favour of its survival. The larger eaglet, now 8 weeks old, was almost fledged, its head golden-brown. It weighed 9 lb, an increase of 9 oz in the week, and I had some difficulty now in weighing the strenuously-objecting bird, which always seemed to get one flailing wing, a clutching, taloned foot or a beak-snapping head out of the weighing bag just as I thought I had it safely in. The whole nest was bedraggled and wet, no attempt at all at freshening it with greenery. This female has definitely no aesthetic sense. A wing of a grouse lay under it, near the dead eaglet.

I weighed the skeleton of the deer calf which had been only hours old when it died, to judge by the still white-edged hooves. It was 5 lb, and covered in flesh it probably had weighed 14 to 15 lb, too heavy I believe to have been carried fully-fleshed into the eyrie. I surmised that one or both adults must have fed on the carcase, where it had been found dead, or had been killed, and in so doing lightened it until it was feasible to lift the remainder into the eyrie. This remains, in twenty years of eagle-watching, the only time I have seen the complete skeleton of a deer calf on any eyrie. More usually it is a portion of the body (often a half, as if severed at mid-joint in the spine), either the hind-quarters or fore-quarters.

On my way back that day the mist was thicker than ever so that I could neither see the female on guard nor could she see me. I groped my way across the ridge by following the line of an old boundary fence, devoutly glad of its aid, for I had once before gone astray on that high-ground plateau in mist, a plateau amazingly featureless under these conditions.

JULY 6TH

The mist, even lower and thicker than last Saturday, spread in an all-embracing, all-obscuring, smoky-grey blanket. Once I left for the hill I could see no more than about six feet ahead of me. I did manage fairly well over the first bit, then inevitably went off-course and had to retrace my steps to a part I could recognise. This time I made as straight as I could judge for the invaluable, rusted and dilapidated boundary fence, and finding it got over the high plateau. It was a major task locating the eyrie and I made a few unsuccessful essays before I eventually came within dim view of a bleached and barkless fallen rowan tree which I knew to lie sprawled below the nest. In the dim world I was walking in I did not see that the female eagle was perched on a branch of the fallen tree, nor did she see me, until I was only a few feet away. She sat facing me, her size accentuated by the mist, and took wing passing straight over my head so that it seemed I could have reached up and touched her. The branch she had left whipped up and down for moments after her take-off, the powerful thrust of her feet as she left imparting a false liveliness to the long-dead wood.

The eaglet was standing in an inner corner of the nest as I arrived, looking fully-fledged now but for fugitive threads of down peeping out here and there among the new feathers. It showed active hostility, for the first time actually advancing across the trampled platform at me, clapping together its wings and striking out with a taloned foot. The nest platform was too damp for the usual cloud of mingled dry dust and feathers to rise off it. Again I had my work cut out weighing it, but finally succeeded, to find it was now $9\frac{1}{2}$ lb, a gain of $\frac{1}{2}$ lb in the week. There was no evidence of prey at the eyrie and no attempt at any freshening with greenery. The mist cleared while I was at the nest, transforming my outlook, literally and metaphorically. Seeing the eaglet cocking one eye skywards, head tilted sideways comically, I too looked up and saw the female patrolling above. Forgetting about her, I went down to the narrow ledge below the nest, where the dead eaglet still lay. It was then the female forcefully reminded me of her presence. A terrifying swoop directly above me as I stooped over the dead eaglet almost panicked me into a wild jump into space. I was so shaken that I reached for my walking-stick and watched her warily as she circled away out of sight above the eyrie crag, to reappear in a minute further out. Banking around at once she made a fast dive at me again, a most impressive sight, wings and body looking immense in their proximity. I prodded upwards with my stick to keep her at a healthy distance, but undaunted, she came around in another fast plunge at me, then flew, to my relief, out of sight to my east. I then went back up to the nest. The light was better and I wanted to photograph the eaglet. The female reappeared as I did so but since I was under the rock overhang which sheltered the actual nest so well, I felt quite safe.

When I finally left the nest she had also disappeared, but I wasn't twenty yards below it when that intimidating swoosh occurred again, as she swooped in from behind. In fact this time I had the hitherto unexperienced sensation of something I had only read about before – of the blood draining from my face, a distinctly unpleasant and quite uncontrollable feeling. Once more she swooped and this last time she came very close indeed making me curse her in no uncertain manner, a sort of safety valve for my own fright and injured feelings. Later she convoyed me along the opposite face but closer than before it seemed, alighting so near to me at times that it would have been suicidal for her had I had a gun and malicious intent towards her. Although I was feeling annoyed and humiliated I did realise she was simply protecting her young and I certainly did not feel like doing anything so drastic as shooting her. As I left under the cover of the mist I surprised a hind which ran off with her two young dappled calves in close attendance. Twins? It certainly seemed so, exceptionally rare though this is with red deer.

JULY 13TH

A fine sunny day at last, rather too warm at times. Fourteen hinds crossed in front of me at one moment and with them five dappled calves. The deer calves were showing more now with their mothers, past the early stage when they had spent much of their time lying alone while the mother grazed elsewhere. High above me I spotted the ever-watchful female eagle as I descended to the bottom of the eagle glen. Approaching the nest from below I could see some grouse feathers which had been caught in its outer structure fluttering in the breeze. When I finally stood at the nest edge I was aghast to find it empty. A very fresh string of grouse entrails suggested that it had been recently vacated. The thick, domed portion of a red deer calf's skull and, attached to it, part of the neck vertebrae, lay on the deserted platform of the nest. Though this had not happened at any eyrie I had been at in the previous years (indeed could not have happened because of their situation), I thought that here the eaglet just might have walked out along the ledge from the nest on to the adjacent hillside, and so I began to climb the face above the eyrie to search for it. I wanted to complete my weighing programme, and to photograph the 10-week-old eaglet.

Suddenly the female swooped, catching me unawares yet again. Two hurried steps took me to the scant shelter of a low rock outcrop, and crouched in the lee of this I took a camera from my bag. Perhaps I could profit from her attacks if she came in again and get vicarious 'revenge' by shooting her on film. I need not have doubted her co-operation for as soon as I straightened up, my head showing just above the rock, she was bearing down on me – fast. Camera to eye, I tried to focus, finding a speck on the viewfinder. Next second the speck was filling it, was through it with tremendous speed, and was gone. She almost disappeared, then banked round and started her incredibly fast run in on me, head sunk low between her shoulders, beak and eyes lined up on me, giant wings now half-folded into her body, legs and feet dropped and held at an angle of about 60°, steely talons dangling, unpleasantly reminiscent of grapnels. Time and again I tried photographing her as she repeatedly and seemingly tirelessly swung in at me but it was frustratingly difficult to synchronise the precise moment when she appeared most distinctly in the viewfinder, the pressing of the camera release, and my own still quite involuntary ducking as she came thundering in. She gave me ample opportunity;

Weighing a recently hatched
eaglet is easy . . .

but a 10-week-old one
is a different matter

After I'd weighed the eaglet it seemed unable to take wing . . .

. . . it stalked awkwardly away

and climbed onto a large boulder which gave it some elevation

Female eagle, head bent down, scrutinising me . . .

. . . swooping at me

and growing in size until she seemed to fill the sky

The common buzzard,
though often
mistaken for an eagle,
is much smaller. It has
a more rounded head
and a slighter beak

The golden eagle is
our largest and most
powerful bird of prey,
with a flatter
looking head and
more impressive beak

The eagle is very vulnerable to being shot when flying off a known eyrie

This huge pole-trap was found as late as 1960 at an eyrie

seen this used in such profusion, and some tufts of long heather, obviously green when taken in, had also, by now, been dried by the sun to a rusty-red.

The first thing I saw, as I eagerly made my last few steps up to the eyrie, was the plucked and headless carcase of a grouse but the cup of this nest was so well tucked in under the shelter of the deep-shelving overhang that I could see no young eagles and experienced a quick pang of dismay. Then I heard familiar weak cheeping. A step or two closer and I was looking in delight at a recently-hatched eaglet sprawled out in the deep nest cup beside an unhatched egg. It had the veiled-eyed look of the very young eagle when the eyes seem to have bulging circular blinkers on them. I was impressed by the beautifully sheltered position of this nest and the more than usually deep cup, warmly-lined, in which eaglet and egg lay, thickly cushioned with great wood-rush. I noticed that the smooth-textured, almost colourless egg, had one or two splotches of red, bloodstains from prey fed to the hatched eaglet. Delighted, I left quickly so as to let the female get back to the nest.

MAY 12TH

I was glad to stretch my legs, walking over to the eyrie after my long drive from Torridon. A pair of red-throated divers were out on the still, black surface of a high lochan and a small lot of red deer ran as I crossed the high plateau. Less welcome was the discovery of a dead deer calf on my way down the face of the eagle glen, a victim of the annual spring mortality which weeds out the weaker 9-month-old calves, and incidently supplies food for the predators in the area. I heard, then saw, a blackface ewe, standing near the glen bottom bleating for a missing lamb, continually. I must admit the first thought that crossed my mind was 'Damn it, has the eagle taken her lamb?'

There was no lamb at the eyrie however and as the ewe was still stubbornly calling when, much later, I left the eyrie, I searched for and finally found her lamb – jammed tight, head-first, in a cranny below a huge rock, out of which it could not reverse. I rescued it, knowing that if I had not been on hand to do so it would have inevitably perished, and its disappearance would have been blamed on eagle or fox.

At the eyrie an adult glided above as I looked at the two eaglets it now held, for the second egg had hatched. One of the tiny, white, down-clad eaglets was markedly smaller and at a week old only weighed $\frac{1}{2}$ lb compared with the older one which scaled 1 lb. The only prey on the nest was the hinder-half of a black water-vole. Below the nest lay a large fragment of thick egg-shell, with its tough, inner, membrane-like skin showing its pale green colour. The eaglets were sleeping in their warm cavity, already shallower in depth than it was last week. They awoke, and were obviously hungry, while I photographed and then weighed them, and began to cheep at me in appeal for food. While I watched the two eaglets, propped upright, thin necks barely holding up over-large heads, the smaller one, in a sudden fit of petulance, suddenly began pecking its larger nestmate with a savagery incongruous in one so small and young. Retribution came swiftly, and in seconds the smaller eaglet lay stretched in subjection, under the rain of ferocious pecks administered by the stronger one. A bad augury for its survival. I left them and went to do a bit of cursory exploring above the nest. As I stood on a knoll above the eyrie I saw an adult eagle come gliding in from the east and suddenly realised she was flying straight at my head. Accustomed as I was by now to the boldness of this particular female this was unexpected because, in the years since 1963, when this female had tried to warn me off she had never started until the eaglets were much older. In she came at a fast glide, losing height and distance rapidly, looming larger and larger while I resisted a compelling urge to duck. I saw her gold head, looking curiously owl-like in expression, with both eyes fixed, unblinking, on me and the dark beak jutting out between them. She was over and past me with a sudden tearing rush of air through stiff pinions. I just had time to note that she had not had her talons down before she was swooping again, now from the west. This time, after her dash at me, a flick of one wing turned her almost at right angles, and she continued her glide right across the glen to her lookout perch on the opposite face.

I saw no deer on the way back but I did see the greenshanks on their usual ridge of the high plateau, where they nest each year.

MAY 18TH

Making my slow way over the high plateau a small narrow-winged bird flicked up near my feet and flew to perch on a knoll ahead. It was a dunlin, its black stomach conspicuous now that I could see it clearly. Like the greenshank, a pair of dunlin, never more, use this area to nest on. The red-throated divers flew off their loch as I went by, a curious humped line to their bodies as they flew. A few yards further on, to my delight, the grey trim shape of a greenshank rose from under my feet. She was so well camouflaged that with my next step forward I would inevitably have stood upon her where she had sat virtually invisible on her eggs. Their pointed ends were arranged to meet neatly in the nest centre, plover fashion.

The female eagle showed herself, gliding from west to east, as I went up the last steep bit to the nest. The eaglets were asleep, with half a grouse, three-quarters of a young mountain hare, and a scattering of black water-vole fur on the nest. Still the marked disparity in size and in weight, 2 lb and almost 1 lb, as in 1963 at this same eyrie.

MAY 26TH

The greenshank was sitting on her nest as I approached but this time, as if aware that her nest had been detected, she left hurriedly before I got too near. Golden plover were intoning their plaintive alarm all around as I crossed from my greenshank ridge to the face above the eagle glen. An eagle soared into the air as I set off down the face, the ever-vigilant female. Below the eyrie I found the hind-leg of a blackface lamb, obviously a puny one. On the actual nest the weaker eaglet lay dead, not white but bloodstained along the entire length of its back, neck and head, quite definitely killed in this case, I believe, by the stronger eaglet. The survivor lay on the ledge beside the haunches of a blackface lamb. One or two small sprigs of rowan cursorily freshened up the nest, which had now become a platform. As I went to weigh the eaglet which was still entirely covered in white down at 3 weeks old it scuttled surprisingly actively back to the nest to lie beside its victim. It now weighed 4 lb whereas the dead one only weighed 1 lb. The female, who had a primary missing from her left wing, came over, on routine inspection only, some half a dozen times before I left the eyrie.

On my way back, as I crossed an area of hummocky heather knolls, intersected by peat runners, a cock grouse suddenly erupted at my feet and snaked forwards a few yards, weaving back and fore, body nearly flattened to the heather. A moment later his mate staged her own weaving and snaking run ahead of me, and there was one, then two, and then three tiny grouse chicks, all lying separate from each other and only saved from my trampling feet by a minor miracle. The hill was certainly coming to life now. A little further on, as I went down the steep incline from the high plateau, a meadow pipit confirmed this, fluttering out from her hidden nest, with a white sac of excrement from her hatched young dangling in her beak.

JUNE IST

The greenshank had hatched and gone; only fragments of eggshell now marked her high-ground nesting place. The plovers were vociferous as usual when I crossed their area and thirty or forty deer were lying high on the green face of the eagle glen, almost opposite the eyrie. The day was dull, but at least it was dry. The female eagle came into view as usual as I went down into the glen. The eaglet was again off the nest, on the green ledge, and beside it lay a half-eaten grouse upon which it had been recently fed, judging by its bulging crop. On the actual nest lay a black water-vole, half-denuded of fur, and a plucked grouse with only its head still feathered. The eaglet was noticeably larger and weighed 6 lb; the 1963 eaglet at this stage had weighed $5\frac{1}{4}$ lb. As I perched on the outer edge of the eyrie, intent on photographing the eaglet, a violent displacement of the air just above me completely destroyed my concentration. Unpredictable as ever, the female had arrived. She repeated her attack twice more while I was at the eyrie. I caught just a lightning glimpse of her dark-brown shape as she shot into view, nearly touching the rock outcrop, banking so steeply that she held her wings in an almost vertical plane, standing on a wing-tip as it were. With the usual rush of air she had sped by and was now flapping wildly with her huge wings to maintain air speed after her plunge at me so near the rock-face. I decided to go to the exposed knoll above the eyrie and see if she would continue attacking. She certainly did and I took at least a score of photographs, when I was quick enough to get a shot of her. In this second position she had no worries about the proximity of the rock-face and I could see her begin the attack-glide from a long way off. At first she was clear against the sky, then momentarily, and a bit nerve-wrackingly, she would vanish as she merged with the hill background so that I never could distinguish just how near she was until she was overhead and away with that great swoosh of air. She did not drop her talons at me any time, as she had done on 13 July 1963, but she did everything else to intimidate me. Twice she rested by perching on a rock only about sixty yards away, twice she made me smile when, flying away from me, she reached forwards in a casual manner with one leg and scratched the back of her head, which she had momentarily turned sideways without a waver in her steady glide. A superb exhibition of flying that gave me great enjoyment. Yet there was always the small niggle of doubt. What if she did come near enough to drop heavily-taloned feet and give me a scalp-tearing rake as she went hurtling by?

Leaving, I came over the top to see only twenty yards away a small herd of twenty-one hinds and their followers, greedily grazing, step by step, on the greens there, bringing my total of deer seen that day to over a hundred, but as yet there were no new calves to be seen.

JUNE 9TH

The greenshanks were very vocal as I crossed their ridge, flying in twisting, flickering darts close by; obviously their chicks were lying crouched somewhere nearby. Hinds as usual were on the high plateau and in the eagle glen but there were still no new calves apparent. Sheep and lambs too were grazing in the glen, a couple of them directly below the eyrie. At the eyrie, a shadow passing overhead told me the female was above and the eaglet confirmed this, peering upwards and cheeping at her. On the eyrie lay the hind-quarters of a mountain hare, a plucked grouse, its crop filled to bulging with fresh green tips of heather, and the eloquent emptiness of a meadow pipit's nest. This must have been plucked, complete and filled with young, from its not quite perfect concealment in a heather or grass tussock and taken to the eyrie, where it now lay empty but still almost as neat as when it had been so painstakingly built. There were one or two sprigs of rowan leaves on the nest and a small tree above the eyrie had had some of its thin uppermost branches freshly broken. The eaglet, at 5 weeks old, weighed 6½ lb and its still mainly white appearance was becoming well speckled with dark feathering. As I halted for a breather on the way back up the steep face opposite the eyrie I saw first one, then the other eagle appear above, to meet, then glide and spiral in unison out over the glen. Seen thus, the female, with her missing primary feather, looked much larger than her neater mate.

For the first time I saw new deer calves – two. I almost trod upon one before it ran from its lying place; the second was running with some fifteen hinds. Will there be deer calf on the eyrie next week, now that these are showing more?

JUNE 16TH

On the drive from Torridon I enjoyed a glimpse of an early morning blackcock, perched on a slender larch leader which looked incapable of sustaining his glossy blue-black bulk. A youngish roe, a yearling doe probably, slipped furtively into wooded cover from a green verge, as always the personification of daintiness, and clumsy-looking brown hares loped over roadside fields near Inverness. A family party of five curlew fluted musically as I crossed a stretch of flat moorland heather after leaving the car. The day was clear now, with wisps of early morning mist fast dispersing. I counted more than ninety deer dotted over hags and hollows on the high plateau but only four dappled calves were showing among that lot. There was deer calf on the nest, the first this season – a clean-picked hind-leg. I had discovered the other hind-leg on the hill-face on my way up to the eyrie. There was also an untouched plucked grouse, and the well-grown eaglet lay off the nest on the green ledge which it seems to prefer as it grows older. It weighed 7¾ lb, obviously well fed and thriving. The female contented herself by periodically patrolling high above without flying low at all. I made myself a can of black sweet tea, as usual, in the glen bottom, over a quick hot fire of dead heather, and while I did so a pair of common gulls, a rare appearance down in this glen, arrived squawking raucously, and one settled confidently on a rock only twelve feet away as if awaiting crumbs from my 'table'. All of a sudden it cocked its white head to one side, comically peering upwards, and equally suddenly took wing, again calling raucously, this time in evident alarm. Looking up I saw the eagle gliding high overhead towards the eyrie-face. As soon as she'd gone the gulls returned to perch, begging, near me. Did they feel safer on the wing, confident in their superior aerial dexterity when an eagle was about, rather than grounded on a rock perch?

The two black-throated divers on the roadside loch had two chicks in convoy. Nearing Torridon, at 11 p.m. on a lovely tranquil evening, the lochs in the glens were polished sheets of jet. A solitary red-throated diver was strikingly mirrored in one. A short-eared owl floating on languid wings, as I drove the final ten miles up Glen Torridon, completed my day.

JUNE 22ND

A flat-squashed tawny owl lay beside an equally squashed brown hare on the road near Muir of Ord. Had the owl been down investigating the fresh-killed hare when, caught unawares, another car had killed it?

I was well down the descent into the eagle glen before the eagle showed but she kept her distance. I stumbled on the single hind-leg of another deer calf as I climbed to the eyrie, and a dead, powerfully-smelling mole lay some distance from it. On the nest lay the two hind-legs of yet another deer calf, cleaned of flesh but still linked together. A half-grown grouse lay on it, untouched as yet, while the 7-week-old eaglet, body well feathered in drab brown but head still mainly in juvenile white, lay in its favourite place on the ledge. It weighed 8 lb, an increase of only $\frac{1}{4}$ lb on last week. A few faded rowan sprays adorned the now tawdry nest platform. On my way back, near where I had seen a pair of grouse and then disturbed a couple of their young-sters, I put up a hen ptarmigan, lovely in her mottled golden-brown and white summer plumage. She snaked enticingly ahead of me while out of the corner of one eye I saw a ptarmigan chick, about the size of the young grouse, rise and flutter a little distance. Lured on by the hen, I followed her for nearly 400 yards before she rose in the never-failing attractiveness of a sudden white blur of wings. I was a little surprised at this apparent overlap of grouse and ptarmigan, yet the altitude was about 2000 feet after all, the usual upper limit for grouse nesting, in my experience, and the lower limit for ptarmigan.

JUNE 29TH

An early morning oyster-catcher led two comically round, down-clad young along the roadside near to Achnasheen. No sign or sound of greenshanks as I crossed their ridge and even the golden plover were less vocal than usual. The female eagle made a token appearance high above as I neared the eyrie but she did not come closer, a quite unpredictable bird. The only prey on the nest was a headless plucked grouse and a few ptarmigan feathers were caught in the structure. The fore-leg of a lamb lay on a ledge below the nest. The eaglet, at 8 weeks old, now intensely disliked being handled and weighed. It weighed 9 lb, and was predominantly dark brown except for the lighter colour of its head and where its well-filled crop bulged, a dirty white, through the brown feathers. I broke up a few of its castings lying below the nest and was intrigued to find the hard shiny wing cases of a black beetle in one.

It was the smallest prey I have so far recorded. No sight of the female as I went up the face from the glen but, as I took a rest, I glanced up towards her guard post and saw a dark, erect finger against the grey rock. Binoculars confirmed that it was the eagle, immobile as a graven image.

JULY 6TH

No sign of grouse or ptarmigan families as I went over the hills, nor of greenshank, but the golden plover were still in evidence, if less exuberant in their alarm. There was a scattering of deer, with some dappled calves now visible among them, all about the eyrie. They obviously had no inherent fear of the proximity of that eyrie. The eaglet had a crop bulging full again and specks of red flesh clung, dried, to its beak. A hind-leg of a deer calf lay on the nest, making a total of four deer calves recorded this season. The eaglet at 9 weeks old was strong on its legs and as it clapped its wings in threat at me dust rose from the brown and withered nest platform. Immaculate-looking in dark brown there were still stray wisps of down to betray its youth. It weighed nearly 9 lb, hardly any increase since last week, typical of the final weeks on the nest. The female did not appear until I had finished weighing the eaglet and again she contented herself with patrolling high above, as if she had now accepted my regular appearances at her eyrie.

I looked for her at her guard post on the opposite face to the eyrie, and was just in time to see her come gliding in and alight on a rock. I saw her change rocks with a clumsy-looking part hop, part scrambling run and, ensconced there, preen herself leisurely with her beak. As she probed among her upper breast feathers a thistledown wisp or two drifted lightly away to become ensnared on a tuft of heather or a rough, lichen-encrusted rock. Her feathers, with their patterns of paler browns and buffs were not nearly as dark as those of her young one. She changed position again and I left her, a still, dark, queenly shape, in possession of *her* glen. I could not help thinking she was much more monarch of what she surveyed than the proudest of red deer stags.

JULY 14TH

When I left Torridon at 5 a.m. it was raining and mist hung low on the hills. There were eleven stags, their antlers well grown in velvet covering and their coats newly red, near the roadside in Glen Torridon and while I stopped to admire them one youngster, with only spikes in velvet, took time off to have a leisurely and apparently enjoyable neck-scratch on a creosoted telegraph pole. Up in the hills the golden plover had at last stopped their plaintive alarm calling. The eagle glen was clear of the mist, and deer, as usual, were dotted about on both faces of the glen. A single oldish-looking hind was lying with three dappled calves, at their ease, spread out in triangle formation beside her. It was tempting to theorise that this old matriarch had been left looking after the nursery, while the mothers grazed, care-free, else-where. There was no sign of prey on the slope below the nest and as I came cautiously up on a level with the nest the eaglet took a couple of quick steps to the outer edge, stood poised magnificently for a second, and launched into space with a swoosh of outstretched wings. It flew, like an expert, out over the glen before turning east; now parallel to the face and gliding fast, it vanished down the glen. Even though I was half expecting it I was still taken aback and, as always, I experienced that feeling of astonishment and admiration at the apparent expertise of the first flight. As it flew, the female appeared, gliding high above, keeping an eye on things. The empty nest platform was flattened and withered but not as compacted as the more usual nest where the occupant has not the advantage of a ledge on which to spend much of its time.

I had marked the eaglet's landing place as well as I could, and hastened after it. Twice I located it and twice more it took wing, the usual pattern, short flights always downwards, till it reached the glen bottom. There I finally caught up with it as it stood, head up, almost disdainful-looking, as if to imply that it had done its best and now didn't give a damn for me anyway. I weighed it, after some beak-snapping protest. It was just 9 lb 1 oz, hardly any gain in the last fortnight on the nest. It looked immaculate – dark-brown, glossy plumage, creamy, buff-striped feather leggings, and copper-brown head with lighter creamy-yellow tips to the feathers. The talons and beak were black and polished, the legs and feet a scaly crayon-yellow. I left it thus, already imperious-looking, while high above the female kept up her watching brief.

1975

I feel it is appropriate to continue with some highlights from the 1975 season when I watched pair C again, on their eyrie E2. On May 3rd I found the two young hatched, and on the nest lay a headless fox cub, a vixen, evoking pity as it lay there, still covered with the blue-grey fur of early cubhood. The weaker eaglet had died by May 11th, with no mark of injury whatever on it. On June 7th another dead fox cub lay on the nest, of about 8 weeks old I would say, a sandy-red colour now. The bloodstained marks on its back, where it had been grabbed by pitiless talons, were glaringly obvious. On May 25th, while having my tea at the glen bottom, I saw first one eagle then the other in the air. They alighted one after the other on the usual guard rock. Through the binoculars I could see them perched close together on the large jutting-out rock. They sat thus for a couple of minutes or so, the sun catching their heads as they turned them this way and that, outlining them in a halo of gold. The female took wing and began to soar, followed by the male, and I was treated to a few minutes of superb flying. At times they were both in my field of vision, spiralling in unison, separating to soar away from each other, then wheeling around to cross and recross each other's path, all without a single wing beat.

On May 31st the female attacked me for the first time in 1975. At this particular eyrie (E2) she did not have to worry about flying close to a cliff-face. I was standing at the nest when I saw her pass high above and moments later that terrific swoosh came as she pulled out from her swoop at me. Attack followed attack at unnerving speed. Turning, so immensely high that she seemed barely more than a speck, she became a black blob, then a hurtling cannon ball, a shape no one in their wildest imagining would associate with an eagle. She was like a huge black vampire bat as she fell rather than flew from the sky, her head hunched between her shoulders, wings folded into the body, legs and taloned feet angled out, fully stretched. Plummeting down she rocked slightly from side to side as she applied correction to her fall. Just as it seemed nothing could prevent her dashing into me, she opened her wings and with that now familiar air-splitting swoosh she pulled out just above my head and away, into the eye of the sun, to rise and bank round, very high, and fly at me once more. It was awe-inspiring, intimidating, fascinating – and absolutely magnificent. No words can hope to do justice to it, that mastery, that power, that control, and that contemptuous pulling out just as it seemed she must dash my head from my shoulders. A revelation beyond words of the unbelievable mastery of an element quite alien to man despite his jet aircraft, Concordes and spacecraft. One slight error of judgement as she neared the eyrie-face, one split second's lack of control, and she would have crashed. I tried not to think that equally a slight mis-timing might send her planing into my head instead of over it. On June 7th she repeated these attacks, and on June 15th and 22nd, that is for four successive weeks. Thereafter with her usual unpredictability she did not attack again during that season. The eaglet, a big bird of 10 lb, flew on July 12th.

The outstanding memory of that year, apart from the eagles, was lying within about twenty feet of a red-throated diver as she sat on her two eggs at the edge of a small island on her high-ground loch. Through my glasses I saw that she was sitting upright on her eggs but, as she became aware of me, she shrank down until she was stretched out flat, her grey, striped, velvety head and neck merging beautifully into the grey rock behind her. I moved cautiously to a rock near the nest and photographed this superb bird. Her wine-red eyes watched my every move but she co-operatively remained on the eggs. These hatched later, but gulls or some other predator got one chick within days, leaving her with only one to rear.

1976

In 1976 I went around the eyrie sites of my four pairs of eagles as usual. I found that pair A had built yet another completely new eyrie in their glen, which already held nine sites. This then was eyrie number ten on their territory, a quite unprecedented number in my experience of eagles. She had laid one egg but my hopes were later dashed for it proved to be addled. Pair B, strangely, were not nesting and since, in later weeks I saw no sign of either adult I came to the conclusion that one, or both, had been victim of trap or poison, possibly accidental in that it may have been intended for fox. Pair D were not nesting either but they have had a consistent record of non-breeding in the last few years. However, I did see both adults in their glen. This, then, was the gloomy picture with one pair, pair C, left to be checked.

MAY 2ND

A grey, drizzly, chilly morning. I left the car at the usual place and took to the hills. The climb up and over the high-ground ridge felt steeper than ever and the weather got colder and wetter as I ascended. Near the top a pair of grouse exploded away, the red-eyebrowed cock making his usual vehement guttural sounds. Only moments later a pair of ptarmigan, grey ghosts of the hill, flew up in dignified silence, a complete contrast to the vulgar noisiness of the grouse. The lochans dotting the top plateau were forbidding expanses, steel-grey, wind-swept and choppy, with only a solitary gull, miserable-looking, huddled at the sheltered end of a small island on one of them. Half a dozen hinds and their yearlings ran from me as I came round into the eagle glen, coats shabby and faded in the old winter hair. Rain obscured the opposite face of the glen where the eyries were and I had to shelter in the lee of a large rock for some time until visibility cleared sufficiently to allow me to examine the eyrie sites. The site she had used last year was quite dead looking, as were the next two. At the nest I had expected her to lay on, however, I was actually able to see the head of an adult eagle. She seemed to be sitting high on the nest and the thought crossed my mind that she had already hatched. The miserable weather was of less consequence now as I crossed over the burn in the glen bottom, stepping-stones awash in the pale-ale colour of the rain-swollen water, and began the final ascent to the eyrie.

The sight of the male eagle, hanging motionless like an over-large kestrel in the air high above the eyrie cliff, reassured me that the eyrie was in use. The female left the nest in a breathtaking display of huge wings when I was only feet from it, leaving two tiny, white, down-clad eaglets, one, typically, much smaller than the other. They reared up unsteadily as I knelt on the eyrie admiring them, and blinked weakly at me. Swaying back and fore, like a couple of cobras to a snake-charmer's pipe, they collided at one moment and in a trice, young as they were, tiny beaks opened and snapped at one another in comical threat. I weighed them before I left. The smaller, only about a day or so hatched, weighed 2 oz, the larger, probably three days hatched, weighed 4 oz. A fragment of grouse was the only prey visible. I stopped in the glen bottom to brew some tea and was able to admire a few red deer, grazing, skylined on the ridge opposite the eyrie, making an attractive frieze. While I was still enjoying my tea, in the peace of the glen, the female eagle returned to her nest and resumed brooding.

MAY 9TH

Climbing up to the eyrie I spotted an erect black shape on the skyline, high above the eyrie – the female, on guard. Under the eyrie ledge lay the discarded remains of a long-billed curlew, new prey to me at an eyrie of the eagle though I had seen curlew as prey at peregrine falcon eyries. The larger eaglet reluctantly opened a sleepy eye, the smaller lay beside it, stretched out as if dead. It was not dead but it was forebodingly weak and it weighed only 8 oz against the 1 lb 4 oz of the larger eaglet. A dead grouse lay on the eyrie yet the crop of the smaller eaglet was empty and it began to cheep weakly for food. The larger, its crop bulging, simply wanted to be left to sleep its meal off. Why had the female, with ample prey on the nest, not fed the weaker eaglet also? I fed it myself, slicing off tiny shreds of grouse and proffering these on the blade of a pen-knife. It eagerly snatched them. After its feed the small bird, weakness dispelled, became almost magically transformed into a lively little chick and it was comical and enlightening to see how it made its way across the wide nest. The legs were at this stage unable to support the weight of the body and so it dug the hooked tip of its tiny beak into the wood-rush lining of the nest and, pulling on this, simultaneously oared itself over the nest with flailing wings. Once it even crossed the somnolent body of its nestmate, without eliciting any protest.

MAY 16TH

Very strong wind had caused groups of red deer to seek shelter in the deep banks of the burn. A look at the eyrie disclosed something white on the ledge just to the east of the nest. When I arrived at the eyrie I found this was the larger eaglet; beside it lay the smaller one, dead. Its back was bloodstained, much of its downy covering had been plucked out and its crop was empty. Its weight was only 12 oz while the survivor weighed 2 lb 6 oz. There is little doubt that it had been killed by the larger eaglet. Searching for signs of prey I found one tiny lower jaw from a fox cub, and just as I was examining this a terrific sound of air being displaced above my head announced that for the first time this season the female eagle had started to serve warning on me. The former warm hollow of the cup of the nest was almost level now, the nest simply a wide platform, the ledge running eastwards forming an extension of this. While I was making tea in the glen below the eyrie the female swooped on a dropping, curving line to a point well below the eyrie and then with beautifully controlled momentum sped up to land lightly on the outer edge of the nest. She sat there for almost an hour, motionless except for her head which she kept turning to look outwards or upwards as if impatiently expecting the arrival of the male hunter with prey and wondering why the devil he was so late. Her head looked alternately dark and pale gold as she turned it this way and that. When she did take wing again the wind was so strong that as she rounded an outcrop high on the face she was literally blown backwards for all of fifty yards, though she kept perfect control throughout.

MAY 22ND

On the way over I saw the pair of red-throated divers on their lochan, riding it out on the windswept surface, so low in the choppy waters that at times they disappeared in the wave troughs. As I approached the eyrie from the glen bottom I noticed, high above the eyrie ridge, the black, winged, silhouette of the male eagle, dwarfed by the distance. Much nearer, the familiar shape of the female, her head gleaming light gold as a stray shaft of sunlight caught it, swept in from down the glen to swing up past the eyrie-cliff and perch on a rock some 400 yards east of the eyrie, an ominous portent. She swooped in repeatedly, so close that at times I had to duck. Once the rasp of feathers on a rock above told me she had misjudged fractionally so that a banking wing-tip had touched the outcrop. At last she desisted and I was able to weigh the eaglet which, for the first time, protested in rapid sibilant cheepings. It weighed $4\frac{1}{4}$ lb. Remains of a lamb and some downy breast feathers from teal or mallard made up the prey today.

MAY 30TH

The eaglet was lying dozing on the nest, the white down of its back sprinkled with dark pinpoints where its first feathers were beginning to sprout. It weighed $5\frac{1}{2}$ lb and protested most vigorously at being weighed. Beside it lay the hind-quarters of a large blue hare. After half an hour at the eyrie without a sign of the female eagle I had ceased thinking of her. Suddenly she swept in, frighteningly close. As if satisfied with the effect of this demonstration she did not repeat it, coming in again only in a rather half-hearted long glide, banking away below the eyrie to reveal the attractive pattern of light browns and shades of buff which constituted the feathers of back and wings, detail which is never apparent when the eagle glides above you, against a background of sky.

Later, resting for a few minutes in the glen bottom, I noticed a sudden and very audible outburst of cheeping from the eyrie some half a mile above. This had been caused by the arrival of the female who simply perched on the outer edge of the eyrie and made no attempt to feed the importunate eaglet on the blue hare remains. Ten minutes she sat there, then flung off again, leaving a most disappointed eaglet.

JUNE 6TH

I spotted a lithe, sandy-red stoat as it whisked across the road ahead of my car, black-tipped tail curving slightly upwards. The female eagle showed up as I climbed to the eyrie. Once, as I watched her vary her tactics by swooping in almost vertically, I was intrigued to see her drop her talons and visibly use them to steer with, and to correct her course, as she fell from the sky in her tremendously fast plunge. The prey consisted of a plucked, headless grouse and one hind-leg of a blue hare. The eaglet was just capable of supporting its weight (now 7 lb) but was still not keen on doing so for long. The plumage was at the piebald stage, half white, half dark, as the new feathers increasingly showed through the down.

Of great interest was the sight of a male hen harrier, unusual in that glen. It flew by, low over the heather banks of the glen bottom, its grey-white, gull-like plumage with conspicuous black wing-tips very distinctive. In unmistakeably languid flight, it passed well below the eyrie but nevertheless poaching flagrantly on the eagle territory. On the way back I stopped on the ridge overlooking the red-throated divers' loch. The resident pair of greenshanks, obviously with recently-hatched young lurking nearby, at once set up a tremendous racket and flew, protesting loudly, up and down the length of the loch, hurtling along, winding and twisting, like wind-blown leaves before a hurricane. At first there was no sight of the red-throats, but minutes later, a single red-throat, the female as it turned out, flew in low over the water landing on the lochan near the usual nest inlet. There she remained, floating as airy as thistledown, gradually drifting nearer to the nest site but the greenshanks, still loudly crying, had made her nervous and she did not get out of the water on to the nest though she obviously wanted to. Once or twice the wind-driven waves of the loch actually washed over her back but it always emerged dry and immaculate, a tribute to her oiled plumage. While I was watching, eager to see her get out on to the nest, the harsh, discordant gabbling of a red-throated diver in flight sounded and the female, as if in answer, lowered her head until it almost touched the water and wailed, twice. The male flew in – a curiously hump-backed outline – head lowered on down-curving neck, short tail also down-curved, broad-webbed feet reaching down and widespread at about a 45° angle on the dark-coloured legs. These webbed feet touched down fractionally before the bird's breast planed forward on the water leaving a V-shaped wake behind. He came to rest neatly, floating beside his mate and, seen together, he was perceptibly larger, with a thicker neck and body than the more svelte female. His throat patch seemed more brilliant than hers, almost a vermilion red compared to her darker shade. After a moment or two of greeting and display during which they aqua-planed side by side over the water, silvery spray flying, the male dived, followed immediately by his mate, and both surfaced almost at the nest edge. The male was the nearer and he also seemed to be the keener to get out on to the nest, yet something seemed to check him at the last moment, perhaps the incessant shrilling of the greenshanks, still at their aerial ballet. Once or twice he half-reared his white breast out of the water at the nest edge, once or twice he elongated his neck and head as if craning to peer at the nest. Now and then he darted his head under water and picked a piece of vegetation, then rubbed it slowly and sensuously along the line of his back feathers. His mate seemed emboldened by his presence, but by the time I had to leave neither had climbed out on to the nest.

JUNE 13TH

A cold, grey and rainy day. The eaglet's back and wings were mostly feathered, in a drab dark brown. Its breast still had a broad central strip of white down stretching from neck to tail. The head was mainly white with streakings of light copper-brown just beginning to colour it. It was strong on its feathered legs and the scaly, black-taloned feet were a deep crayon-yellow. It was now $6\frac{1}{2}$ weeks old and weighed, under protest, $7\frac{1}{2}$ lb.

JUNE 20TH

Coming around on to the green face of the eagle glen two startled hinds jumped up and ran from me. A few steps further on I almost stood upon a dappled calf, no more than a couple of days old, lying tucked up snugly out of the wind. I could almost see it making up its mind to run for it as I stared in admiration, the apprehension building up in its heaving, creamy-dappled flanks until, suddenly, it was up and away, almost tripping over its own crossed forelegs in juvenile haste. To the west, further up the glen, both adult eagles were visible in the sky, leisurely wheeling around on set wings. Would they see the tiny calf running and would they attack? Indeed, how could they fail to see the moving calf on that bare green hill-face. For

119

long moments the suspense endured; then it became clear that no attack was coming. The calf ran unscathed until, tired, it lay down in some other nook further up the glen. Crossing a little gully almost opposite the eyrie, before making the final descent to the glen below, I saw a dead hind sprawled out below me. At once suspecting a calving casualty I went down to investigate; occasionally a red deer hind will have trouble in giving birth to her calf in June and both hind and calf may die. It was difficult to tell in this case, she was a day or two dead and already the eagles had stripped the flesh off most of her hind-quarters and her unborn calf, if there had been one, was gone. And then I spotted one small milk-tooth molar lying among scattered hairs by the dead hind. So there had been a double tragedy, yet in this natural death, and the consequent feeding for the eagles, may have lain the saving of a healthy deer calf or two, perhaps including the one ignored by the eagles only half an hour ago.

Below the eyrie I found a discarded fore-leg of a red deer calf, all flesh cleaned off it, the first calf seen this season as prey. On the eyrie itself there was only a trace of black water-vole fur and a bit of grouse. The eaglet, almost entirely covered in sober dark brown with its lighter head feathers in copper-brown, was quite aggressive, striking with beak and talons. Despite this I weighed it and at $7\frac{1}{2}$ weeks old it scaled 9 lb, an impressive weight for an increasingly impressive bird.

JUNE 27TH

A very strong south-west wind made progress over the high ridge laborious. No red deer at all on the wind-scourged top but a herd of thirty-seven hinds was gathered, well tucked in out of the wind, in a gully at the head of the eagle glen, and as they ran I could see seven tiny dappled calves with them. Below the eyrie I again picked up the fore-leg of a calf; another leg lay on the nest, the second calf as prey this season. The head of the 8½-week-old eaglet was not quite fully feathered but its body plumage was nearly complete, though stubborn wisps of down still stuck out haphazardly through the dark brown. It objected most strenuously, with flailing wings, snapping beak and clutching talons, to being weighed but at last this was accomplished. Still 9 lb, no increase in the past week. The female only made a token appearance.

JULY 4TH

A yearling roe doe, panic-stricken on hearing the car, raced back and forth along a roadside fence, barging into it, trying to force a way through it when she could so easily and gracefully have cleared it in one bound. A little further on a mature roe doe tip-tapped her way across the road ahead of the car, unhurriedly. Behind her, irresistibly appealing, tripped a sandy-red, faintly dappled miniature, her young fawn. No panic here, they disappeared quietly into the roadside trees and the brief enchantment was gone. For once this year the climb across the top was a warm one and a cooling wind would have been welcome. I was nearly at the eyrie before the female appeared, gliding low above me, but not in attack. The eaglet, lying on the inner edge of the eyrie, sprang to its feet on my arrival and took two long strides across to the outer edge of the eyrie so that I expected it to launch out into space. But no, it halted there and began a querulous high-pitched yelping which it kept up for at least ten minutes. Grouse remains and the velvety black-furred carcase of a water-vole lay on the nest. There was no deer calf in evidence. The eaglet was now an extremely elegant and trim-looking bird, only a very few elusive threads of down visible among the dark feathers. Apparently determined to show me that she was still to be reckoned with, the female came swooping in at me three times, then abruptly desisted. The first time the attack was so sudden that she made even the eaglet jump in alarm. When I finally succeeded in weighing the violently struggling eaglet I was surprised to find it had lost a $\frac{1}{4}$ lb in the week, it was now only $8\frac{3}{4}$ lb. Trimmed down to flying weight? By its neatness and relatively light weight at this stage I suspected it was a male bird. I left it perched proudly on the eyrie's edge, looking across the glen it would shortly fly over, its poise and dignity regained after the weighing ordeal. I wondered if I would see it on the eyrie on July 11th?

JULY 11TH

The eyrie was empty, a deserted, trampled-flat platform with a host of downy wisps of juvenile preening caught in and around its structure. A few small adult feathers spoke of preening by the female. One or two bare breast bones of grouse lay on it, a scrap of black water-vole fur and a wisp of blue hare fur. It was a withered structure, desolate in its emptiness after long weeks of occupancy but it was not in the least foul, neither to the eye nor to the nose. I judged the eaglet to have been gone for at least three to four days, at around ten weeks after hatching, in fact, the usual leaving stage in this glen.

My final sight in this glen was of an eagle flying west up the glen, using rather more wing flaps than is usual, but none the less flying well enough for a learner. As I watched, a larger eagle came gliding fast on set wings towards me, only to soar up before reaching me and land on her favourite cliff guard post, opposite her eyrie across the glen. It was the vigilant female, now with her charge airborne, but still covering his retreat. And so I left them for another year.

It may not be generally realised that even when an eaglet has safely flown from an eyrie the parents' responsibilities are by no means over. For a further three months or so they will look after the eaglet, part feeding it until it is skilful enough to catch its own prey, teaching it to catch this prey and to cope generally with existence. By early October usually the eaglet will leave the parents' territory. Whether voluntarily or actually driven off remains surmise. These single birds may be seen wintering in areas not generally regarded as eagle territory and in their first winter and spring carrion will no doubt form an important part of their diet. Grallochs of deer shot in the stalking season will also be eaten. I have flushed eagles off these, and once the carcase of a hind left out overnight was partly stripped of flesh by an eaglet who could hardly take off from the tree where he was perched in a state of torpor after his enormous meal. There is probably a significant mortality rate in these juveniles who do not learn to feed themselves quickly enough. The survivors, who are of breeding age at four years old, form a pool from which deceased breeding adults are replaced as the need arises.

I discovered in July 1976 that they may range widely in their immature years when Sandy Masson, stalker at Mamore deer forest, Kinlochleven (near Fort William in Inverness-shire) telephoned me saying he had inadvertently caught a ringed golden eagle in a cage trap set for hooded crows. I drove over to find a fine healthy male bird, with beautiful, rather dark plumage. It weighed 8 lb. We noted the number of the leg ring, then released the eagle and watched it disappear over a ridge a mile away. It proved to have been ringed in 1975 as a nestling in the Loch Lomond area, almost at the southern fringe of the Highlands.

Though I learned much of eagle behaviour over the years, inevitably questions remain. The most puzzling is why have two pairs, B and C, of four adjacent pairs of eagles, with nesting and hunting territories in identical terrain, with the same sort of land use (mainly sheep farming and deer stalking), had consistently better breeding success since the early 1960s than the other two pairs, A and D? (see Appendix.)

Was it a higher degree of contamination by pesticidal residues, ingested by eating carrion in the form of dead sheep? If so why were these two pairs affected more than the other two? A difference in eating habits, or in the sheep dips used? Frankly, I just do not know. Was it, possibly, old age and a decline in the ability to breed in the case of A and D, as compared with B and C? If so it would seem that the female was not to blame for from the data I had accumulated it seemed all four females were in more or less the same age group. In pair A I had reason to believe that the female had been the victim of poison in 1960 and if we assume the replacement female in 1961 to be, say, 5 years old (eagles are 4–5 years old before they arrive at breeding age) then she is, in 1976, 20 years old. In pair B the female was shot in 1962 and, on a similar assumption, her replacement in 1963 is now 18 years old. Pair C's female was shot in 1959 so, again, her replacement in 1960 is now 21 years old. This female I know particularly well and her behaviour pattern is unmistakeable. Pair D lost its female (shot on the nest as were B and C) in 1961, and following the same premiss, she is now 19 years old. There is always the possibility that the females of A and D were older birds when they replaced the defunct ones but I believe it is much more likely and logical that all the replacements came from a floating population of immature or near immature single birds. If it is old age and decline in breeding powers on the part of one of the pair in A and D then it seems it must be the male. During the nesting season the male is always less vulnerable to shooting (as practised yearly not so very long ago in many areas) than the female.

Other aspects of eagle behaviour pose questions: why should pair A, with already more eyrie sites to choose from than is usual, continue to build on new sites, as she did again this year (1976), so that there are now ten eyrie sites in their glen, an unprecedented number in one nesting glen to my knowledge. And why did pair B, with a choice of two other sites, elect to use the same site (E1) in two successive years, 1969 and 1970, to rear successfully on? Similarly, why did pair C, with a choice of five other sites, use the same site (E2) in three successive years, 1970, 1971 and 1972, to rear successfully on? Why did pair A never lay more than one egg in the 20-year period, though at least three different females were involved, while the other three pairs had the usual clutch of two eggs? Why was the female of pair C so consistently aggressive over the years, not at all typical of eagle behaviour, while the female of pair B was, to say the least, most unobtrusive while one was visiting her eyrie?

It may be that these examples of seemingly individualistic behaviour or pattern simply underline my belief that it is unwise to generalise too completely on the behaviour, instincts and patterns of wildlife. Among animals and birds there would seem to be individuals, just as in humans – and why not.

One fact seems certain: the reproduction rate of our golden eagles is by no means high. Against this there remains the threat of illegal egg collecting, of the illegal removal of young eagles from the nest allegedly for falconry, and the now more sporadic but still present threat of totally illegal persecution by a few diehard grouse preservers and, at times, hill sheep farmers. There is also the very real danger posed by the all too widespread and illegal use of poison throughout the Highlands as a means of control on the numbers of foxes and hooded crows. When used, as it often is, in dead rabbit, sheep or deer this poison is as likely to kill a carrion-eating eagle as the fox or crow for which it may have been designed. If we are to continue to have the golden eagle with us as a breeding species we must continue to be vigilant and to employ every means we can to encourage its protection.

Appendices

APPENDIX I

BREEDING SUCCESS IN 4 PAIRS OF EAGLES: A, B, C & D

PAIR A
(10 Eyrie Sites, E1 to E10)

YEAR	RESULT	EYRIE SITE
1957	Female shot on nest	E1
1958	One eaglet reared	E1
1959	One eaglet reared	E7
1960	Female believed poisoned	—
1961	One eaglet reared	E8
1962	One sub-standard egg, addled	E1
1963	No breeding	—
1964	No breeding	Pair seen in glen
1965	No breeding	Pair seen in glen
1966*	No breeding	—
1967	No breeding	Pair seen in glen
1968	One egg, addled	E1
1969	One eaglet reared	E4 (*new site*)
1970	No breeding	One eagle seen in glen
1971	No breeding	One eagle seen in glen
1972	No breeding	One eagle seen in glen
1973*	No breeding	Pair seen in glen
1974	One eaglet hatched, disappeared later	E8 (*new nest* only feet from old one on the site)
1975	No breeding	—
1976	One egg laid, addled	E3 (*new site*)

Known number reared over study period = 4
Incidence of two reared in a season = 0
    N.B. This pair only had one egg in clutch
Favourite site: E1

* 100% breeding failure years. No eaglets reared in any of the 4 pairs.

Breeding Success in 4 Pairs of Eagles

PAIR B
(3 Eyrie Sites, E1 to E3)

YEAR	RESULT	EYRIE SITE
1957	No record	—
1958	Female shot	E1
1959	Female shot	E2
1960	Two eaglets reared	E3
1961	Two eaglets reared	E1
1962	Female shot	E2
1963	One eaglet reared	E1
1964	One eaglet reared	E3
1965	One eaglet reared	E1
1966*	No breeding	—
1967	One eaglet reared	E1
1968	One eaglet reared	E2
1969	Two eaglets reared	E1
1970	One eaglet reared	E1
1971	One eaglet reared	E3
1972	Only one egg, addled	E2
1973*	Eggs laid, addled	E1
1974	Eggs laid, addled	E1
1975	One eaglet reared	E1
1976	No breeding. Adult/s poisoned?	—

Known number reared over study period = 14
Incidence of two reared in a season = 3
    N.B. This pair usually had two eggs in clutch
Favourite site: E1

* 100% breeding failure years. No eaglets reared in any of the 4 pairs.

Breeding Success in 4 Pairs of Eagles

PAIR C
(6 Eyrie Sites, E1 to E6)

YEAR	RESULT	EYRIE SITE
1957	No record	—
1958	No record	—
1959	Female shot	E2
1960	No record	—
1961	No record	—
1962	One eaglet reared	E4
1963	One eaglet reared	E5
1964	Two eggs, disappeared before hatched	E2
1965	One eaglet hatched, later disappeared	E4
1966*	No breeding	—
1967	One eaglet reared	E5
1968	Two eaglets reared	E1 (*new site*)
1969	Two eggs, one addled, one disappeared	E5
1970	Two eaglets reared	E2 ⎫ N.B. Used
1971	One eaglet reared	E2 ⎬ in three
1972	One eaglet reared	E2 ⎭ successive years
1973*	Two hatched. Killed at month old, human interference	E5
1974	One eaglet reared	E5
1975	One eaglet reared	E2
1976	One eaglet reared	E5

Known number reared over study period = 12
Incidence of two reared in a season = 2
    N.B. This pair usually had two eggs in clutch
Favourite sites: E2 and E5

---

* 100% breeding failure years. No eaglets reared in any of the 4 pairs.

Breeding Success in 4 Pairs of Eagles

PAIR D
(4 Eyrie Sites E1 to E4)

YEAR	RESULT	EYRIE SITE
1957	No record	—
1958	No record	—
1959	One eaglet reared	E2
1960	One eaglet reared	E3
1961	Female shot on nest	E4
1962	One eaglet reared	E1
1963	No breeding	—
1964	One egg, addled	E1
1965	Two eggs, addled	E1
1966*	Two eggs, addled	E2
1967	One egg, addled	E1
1968	No breeding	—
1969	Two eggs, addled	E1
1970	No breeding	—
1971	Two eggs, addled	E1
1972	Two eggs, addled	E2
1973*	No breeding	One eagle seen
1974	No breeding	—
1975	No breeding	Pair seen in glen
1976	No breeding	Pair seen in glen

Known number reared over study period = 3

Incidence of two reared in a season = 0

N.B. This pair usually had two eggs in clutch

Favourite site: E1

Known overall result over study period from 4 pairs = 33 eaglets reared

* 100% breeding failure years. No eaglets reared in any of the 4 pairs.

APPENDIX II

WEIGHTS OF EAGLETS, HATCHING TO FLYING STAGE,
WEIGHED WEEKLY IN 1963, 1974, 1975 AND 1976 (PAIR C)

1963

May 4th	Two eggs, one in process of hatching	
May 11th	Smaller eaglet 8 oz	larger eaglet 1 lb
May 18th	Smaller eaglet 1 lb	larger eaglet almost 2 lb
May 25th	Smaller eaglet 2 lb	larger eaglet 4 lb
June 1st	Smaller eaglet 2½ lb	larger eaglet 5¼ lb
June 8th	Smaller eaglet 4 lb	larger eaglet 7 lb
June 15th	Smaller eaglet 5 lb	larger eaglet 8 lb 6 oz
June 22nd	Smaller eaglet 4½ lb*	larger eaglet 8 lb 7 oz
June 29th	Smaller eaglet DEAD	larger eaglet 9 lb
July 6th	—	larger eaglet 9 lb 8 oz
July 13th	—	larger eaglet 9 lb 12 oz

1974

May 5th	One egg	one hatched eaglet 2 oz
May 12th	Smaller eaglet 8 oz	larger eaglet 1 lb
May 19th	Smaller eaglet 1 lb	larger eaglet 2 lb
May 26th	Smaller eaglet DEAD	larger eaglet 4 lb
June 1st	—	larger eaglet 6 lb
June 9th	—	larger eaglet 6½ lb
June 16th	—	larger eaglet 7¾ lb
June 22nd	—	larger eaglet 8 lb
June 29th	—	larger eaglet almost 9 lb
July 6th	—	larger eaglet 9 lb
July 14th	—	larger eaglet 9 lb 1 oz

* Note ½ lb loss in weight.

Weights of Eaglets

1975

May 3rd	Both hatched, smaller 2 oz,	larger 4 oz
May 11th	Smaller eaglet DEAD 5 oz	larger eaglet 12 oz
May 18th	—	larger eaglet $2\frac{1}{4}$ lb
May 25th	—	larger eaglet $4\frac{1}{4}$ lb
May 31st	—	larger eaglet 6 lb
June 7th	—	larger eaglet $7\frac{1}{4}$ lb
June 15th	—	larger eaglet $8\frac{3}{4}$ lb
June 22nd	—	larger eaglet $9\frac{1}{4}$ lb
June 28th	—	larger eaglet 10 lb
July 5th	—	larger eaglet 10 lb
July 12th	—	Flew from eyrie, assume around 10 lb

1976

May 2nd	Both hatched, smaller 2 oz,	larger 4 oz
May 9th	Smaller eaglet 8 oz	larger eaglet 1 lb 4 oz
May 16th	Smaller eaglet DEAD 12 oz	larger eaglet 2 lb 6 oz
May 23rd	—	larger eaglet $4\frac{1}{4}$ lb
May 30th	—	larger eaglet $5\frac{1}{2}$ lb
June 6th	—	larger eaglet 7 lb
June 13th	—	larger eaglet $7\frac{1}{2}$ lb
June 20th	—	larger eaglet 9 lb
June 27th	—	larger eaglet 9 lb
July 4th	—	larger eaglet $8\frac{3}{4}$ lb*

* Note $\frac{1}{4}$ lb loss in weight.

134

APPENDIX III

Red deer calf
Lamb
Fox
Blue hare
Rabbit
Stoat
Black water-vole
Bank-vole
Mole
Black beetle

Grouse
Ptarmigan
Raven
Hooded crow
Carrier pigeon
Common gull
Curlew
Teal
Nestling ring ousel
Meadow pipit (nest presumably plucked out of its site in a heather bank and brought in full of young pipits)

APPENDIX IV

Bearberry
Birch
Blaeberry
Crowberry
Grass (a clod with earth attached)
Heather
Juniper
Moss (*Bartramia pomiformis*)
Moss (*Racomitrium*)
Moss (*Sphagnum*)
Scots pine
Common rush
Great wood-rush
Dwarf willow
Rowan

BIBLIOGRAPHY

BANNERMAN, D. A.   *The Birds of the British Isles* (Oliver & Boyd, Edinburgh 1956)

CONWAY, J.   *Forays Among Salmon and Deer* (Chapman & Hall, London 1861)

CREALOCK, H. H.   *Deerstalking* (Longmans Green & Co Ltd, London 1892)

DIXON, J. H.   *Gairloch*, 1886 (reprint 1974 Ross and Cromarty Heritage Society)

ELLICE, E.   *Placenames of Glengarry* (Routledge & Kegan, London 1931)

GORDON, S.   *The Golden Eagle* (Collins, London 1955)

MILLAIS, J. G.   *British Deer and Their Horns* (H. Southeran, London 1897)

MORTIMER BATTEN, H.   *British Wild Animals* (Odhams, London 1952)

ST JOHN, C.   *Sport and Natural History of Morayshire* (David Douglas, Edinburgh 1863)

SPEEDY, T.   *The Natural History of Scotland with Rod and Gun* (Blackwoods, Edinburgh 1920)

STALKER, AN OLD   *Days on the Hill* (Nisbet and Co, Welwyn 1926)

137

Index

Index